Dr. Fry's

Beginning Writers Manual

Spelling Checker, Grammar Rules and Suggested Topics

by Edward Fry, Ph.D.
&
Elizabeth Sakiey, Ed.D.

Y0-CAX-697

Beginning Writers Manual Spelling Checker, Grammar Rules and Suggested Topics

by **Edward Fry, Ph.D**
Professor Emeritus
Rutgers University
&
Elizabeth Sakiey, Ed.D.
Professor of Reading
Rowan College of N. J.

Teacher Created Materials, Inc.
6421 Industry Way
Westminster, CA 92683
www.teachercreated.com

ISBN-1-57690-759-7

©1995, Edward Fry, Ph.D.
Laguna Beach Educational Books

Reprinted, 2000
Made in U.S.A.

TABLE OF CONTENTS

TABLE OF CONTENTS *(cont.)*

INTRODUCTION

Beginning Writers Manual is valuable resource book, designed to assist beginning writers whether they are students in elementary or secondary school or adults.

This manual is useful to have in the classroom (and at home) as a quick reference to common spellings and basic usage rules. Preferably, students will have their own copy, or at least several copies will be readily available in each classroom.

Beginning Writers Manual is divided into eight major sections as described briefly below. Because many of these can be developed into whole lessons, a section entitled "Teaching Suggestions" is included on pages 7–9.

Take a few minutes and look over each of the sections in this book. Then use the "Teaching Suggestions" to acquaint students with this manual, showing them how to find needed information. Let your students know that even very experienced writers use reference books to look up the spelling of words or the proper punctuation. The important thing is knowing where to find information.

1. Spelling Checklist

The first and largest portion of this book is a list of nearly 7,000 words commonly used in writing. This list can be used to check spelling and is faster than using a dictionary because there are more words on a page and the common variants (like irregular plurals, participles, and adjective forms) are listed under the root word.

2. Personal Spelling List

Next is a section called "Personal Spelling List," which writers can use to keep a list of words they have trouble spelling (words that are not in the "Spelling Checklist").

3. Spelling Rules

Guidelines related to plurals, prefixes, suffixes, compound words, and phonics are included in this section, as well as a table of common abbreviations.

4. Grammar

This section contains grammar basics and focuses on the construction of sentences, parts of speech, and rules for capitalization and punctuation.

5. Types and Uses of Writing

The different kinds of writing are summarized here, and guidelines are offered for writing letters, book reports, story summaries, and journals.

6. The Writing Process

Writers are guided through the four stages of the writing process (prewriting, writing, revising, and proofreading) in this section.

7. Story Starters

In this section, writers are provided with ideas for titles, opening sentences, questions, and endings to help them get started.

8. Jazz Up Your Writing

This section gives tips for improving one's vocabulary and also includes a description of literary terms, which can enrich any writer's style

TEACHING SUGGESTIONS

To help students learn how to effectively use this book, suggested drills have been included. Most of these drills can be oral or written and done with the entire class, a small group, or even individual tutoring.

The drills serve two main purposes. The first is to familiarize students with the contents of the book and where things are located. The second is to develop speed in locating the information.

The first few drills involve alphabetization and require a lot of practice. Drill your students several times a week for several weeks to develop speed and accuracy. Give extra drills to slower students. Use praise or other rewards for students who are fastest, most accurate, have just caught on, or who are making progress.

It's important to transfer the skills learned in these drills to real-life situations. For example, if a student asks how to spell a word or turns in a paper with spelling errors, have him look up words in the "Spelling Checklist." If a student turns in a paper with incorrect punctuation or grammar, refer him to the section in this book that contains the needed information.

Each of the sections of the *Beginning Writers Manual* provides the content for many lessons. For example, the section on "Spelling Rules" suggests lessons on the spelling of plurals or doubling the final letter when adding a suffix, and the "Punctuation" section suggests lessons on using commas and apostrophes.

Spelling Checklist: Guide Letters (pages 11–68)

Using just the letters at the top of the page, quickly find just the page on which each of the following words are located. Give the page number.

- wheel
- obtain
- February

(Note: For this drill, don't take time to locate the word on the page. The purpose is to learn to use the guide letters at the top of the page.)

Spelling Checklist: Alphabetization (pages 11–68)

Now find the following words, using first the guide letters at the top of the page, then the two letter word group heading in the page. Give the word just before each.

- eagle
- Sweden
- polar

Spelling Checklist: Variant Forms (pages 11–68)

What other word forms are in the word list for each of these base words?

- beg
- Spain
- vote

Spelling Checklist: Homophones (pages 11–68)

What other words have the same sound but different meanings as each of these words?

- for
- weigh
- do

Personal Spelling List (pages 69–75)

Name three kinds of words that should be added to a personal spelling list.

Spelling Rules: Plurals (pages 76)

How do you spell the plural of the following words?

- fox
- candy
- knife

Spelling Rules: Suffixes (pages 78–79)

Spell the words that result from adding the following suffixes to each root word.

- nose + y
- marry + ed
- hit + ing

Spelling Rules: Phonics (page 82)

What are three ways the Long A sound can be spelled?

Spelling Rules

Abbreviations (pages 86–92)

What are the abbreviations for each of the following?

- Maine
- foot
- a married woman
- centimeter
- Monday
- adverb

Grammar: Parts of Speech (pages 98–99)

What part of speech is each of the following words?

- man
- beautifully
- run
- and
- beautiful
- he

Grammar: Sentences (pages 100–103)

Change this sentence, "I can do my homework"

- into a negative sentence.
- into a question.
- into passive voice.

Grammar: Verbs (pages 105–108)

Correct the following verb errors:

- She sing very well.
- She sing yesterday.
- She sing tomorrow.
- She sing in the shower now.

Grammar: Capitalization (pages 110–111)
Name three kinds of words that need to be written with a capital letter.

Grammar: Punctuation (pages 112–115)
1. What are three times you need to use a period?
2. What are the three main uses of an apostrophe?

Types and Uses of Writing (page 116)
Name three different types of writing.

Types and Uses of Writing: Letter Forms (pages 117–118)
How does a business letter differ from a friendly letter?

Types and Uses of Writing: Book Report (page 119–120)
How does the form for a book report differ from that of a story map?

Types and Uses of Writing: Journal Keeping (pages 121–122)
Name three different things you might write about in a journal.

The Writing Process (pages 123–130)
What are the four stages in the writing process?

The Writing Process: Proofreading Symbols (page 131)
What is the symbol for making a new paragraph?

Story Starters (pages 132–135)
Give one original idea for each of the following:

- interesting title
- opening sentence
- great question
- story endings

Jazz Up Your Writing: Vocabulary Improvement (page 136)
What are three ways to improve one's vocabulary?

Jazz Up Your Writing: Literary Terms (pages 137–141)
Give an original example for each of the following terms:

- alliteration
- hyperbole
- contraction
- idiom
- antonym
- metaphor

SPELLING CHECKLIST

The following pages contain a list of nearly 7,000 words commonly used in writing. Using this list to check spelling is faster than using a dictionary because there are more words on a page and the common variants (like irregular plurals, participles, and adjective forms) are also listed under the root word. For example, under the entry "administer" are the words "administration" and "administrator." Irregular verbs, those which do not follow the usual inflected form, include the notation "(irreg. vb.)".

In addition, homophones are listed in brackets under their corresponding words with a brief definition for each. For example, under the listing for "right (correct)" are the entries "[rite (ceremony)]" and "[write (inscribe)]". Words that are often confused are also listed together in brackets with a brief definition (examples: affect and effect, precede and proceed).

Words are alphabetically arranged under two-letter subheads; this makes it easier to locate words. For example, the words "rub," "rude," "rule," and "ruler" (plus others) are found under the subhead ru.

Words with regular suffixes (-ed, -er, -est, -ful, -ing, -less, -ly, -ness, -s) are not in the "Spelling Checklist" because they can be added to the end of a word without changing the spelling of the combined root word and suffix.

Words that require a change in spelling when a suffix is added are listed under their root word in the "Spelling Checklist." Plural forms of words are also listed if the spelling is atypical (requires more than an "s"). These exceptions include doubling the final consonant before adding the suffix (example: run - running) and using "es" to form the plural (example: church - churches). A footnote to this regard appears on alternate pages and will serve as a reminder.

Consequently, a student should first look up the root word in the "Spelling Checklist." If the user needs a variant form using a regular ending, it can just be added (example: accent - accented - accents). If the root word or ending is spelled differently, it will be listed under the root word (example: admit - admitted - admitting - admission).

The words in this checklist are from a scientifically-determined list of 3,000 of the most frequently-used words in the English language and their common variants, plus familiar words chosen from the *Random House School Dictionary*. Although this list is not all the words needed by a beginning writer, it consists of over 95% of the words used by writers of any age.

a

a

ab

ability
   abilities
able
   abler
   ablest
   ably
aboard
about
above
absent
absorb

ac

accent
accept *(to receive)*
   [except *(to exclude)*]
accident
   accidental
accommodate
   accommodated
   accommodating
accompany
   accompanied
   accompanies
   accompaniment
account
   accountant
accurate
   accuracy
ache
   ached
   aching
achieve
   achieved
   achiever
   achieving
   achievement
acid
acorn
acre
acrobat
   acrobatic
across
act
   action
   active
   activities

activity
actor
actress
actual

ad

ad *(advertisement)*
   [add *(find the sum)*]
adapt
add *(find the sum)*
   [ad *(advertisement)*]
   adds *(combines)*
   [ads *(advertisement)*]
   [adz *(ax-like tool)*]
addition
   additional
addend
   addenda
addict
address
adjective
adjust
admire
administer
administration
   administrator
admit
   admission
   admitted
   admitting
adopt
   adoption
ads *(advertisement)*
   [adds *(combines)*]
   [adz *(ax-like tool)*]
adult
advance
   advanced
   advancer
   advancing
advantage
adventure
   adventured
   adventurer
   adventuresome
   adventuring
   adventurous
adverb
advice
adz *(ax-like tool)*
   [adds *(combines)*]
   [ads *(advertisement)*]

af

affair
affect *(to influence)*
   [effect *(the result)*]
affection
   affectionate
afford
afraid
Africa
   African
after
   afternoon
   afterward

ag

again
   against
age
   aged
   aging
agent
ago
aggravate *(make worse)*
   [agitate *(stir up)*]
agree
   agreed
   agreement
agriculture
   agricultural
   agriculturally

ah

ah
ahead

ai

aid *(help)*
   [aide *(assistant)*]
ail *(be sick)*
   [ale *(beverage)*]
aim
air *(what you breathe)*
   [heir *(successor)*]
airplane
airport
aisle *(narrow path)*
   [I'll *(I will)*]
   [isle *(island)*]

al

Alabama
alarm
Alaska
   Alaskan
alcohol
   alcoholic
ale *(beverage)*
   [ail *(be sick)*]
alike
alive
all *(everything)*
   [awl *(pointed tool)*]
alley
alligator
allow
   allowed *(permitted)*
   [aloud *(audibly)*]
ally
   allied
   allies
   allying
almost
alone
along
aloud *(audibly)*
   [allowed *(permitted)*]
alphabet
   alphabetic
   alphabetical
   alphabetize
already *(previously)*
   [all ready *(completely prepared or ready)*]
also
altar *(raised church table)*
   [alter *(change)*]
although
altitude
altogether *(completely)*
   [all together *(in a group)*]
aluminum
always

am

am *(irreg. vb.)*
amaze
   amazed
   amazing
America
   American

among
amount
amuse
   amused
   amusing

an

an
ancestor
anchor
ancient
and
angel
anger
angle
   angled
   angler
   angling
angry
   angrier
   angrily
animal
announce
   announced
   announcer
   announcing
annoy
annual
another
answer
ant *(insect)*
   [aunt *(parent's sister)*]
anxious
any
anybody
anyone
anything
anyway *(adverb)*
   [any way *(adjective and noun)*]
anywhere

ap

apart
apartment
apology
apostrophe
apparent
appeal
appear
   appearance

apple
apply
   applicable
   applicant
   application
   applicative
   applicator
   applicatory
   applied
   applier
   applies
appoint
   appointee
approach
   approaches
appropriate
approve
   approved
   approving
   approvingly
approximate
   approximated
   approximately
April
apron

ar

Arab
   Arabian
   Arabic
arc *(arched curve)*
   [ark *(a boat)*]
arch
Arctic
are *(irreg. vb.)*
area
aren't *(are not)*
Argentina
argue
   argument
   argumentative
arithmetic
Arizona
ark *(a boat)*
   [arc *(arched curve)*]
Arkansas
arm

The following regular endings are not in the word list and can be added to the root word without changes:
-ed, -er, -est, -ful, -ing, -less, -ly, -ness, and -s. Most exceptions and root changes are in the list.

ar *(cont.)*

army
  armies
around
arrange
  arranged
  arranger
  arranging
  arrangement
arrive
  arrival
  arrived
  arriving
arrow
art
article
artist
  artistic
  artistically

as

as
ascend
  ascension
ascent *(a climb)*
  [assent *(agree)*]
ash
  ashes
Asia
  Asian
aside
ask
asleep
assemble
  assembly
  assemblies
assent *(agree)*
  [ascent *(a climb)*]
assist
  assistance *(help)*
  [assistants *(those who help)*]
associate
  associated
  associating
  association
assume
  assumed
  assuming
astronaut
astronomy
  astronomer
  astronomical

at

at
ate *(did eat)*
  [eight *(the number 8)*]
Atlantic
atmosphere
  atmospheric
atom
  atomic
attach
  attaches
attack
attempt
attend
  attendance *(being present)*
  [attendants *(escorts)*]
attention
attitude
attract
  attractive

au

audience
August
aunt *(parent's sister)*
  [ant *(insect)*]
aural *(of the ears)*
  [oral *(by way of mouth)*]
Australia
  Australian
Austria
  Austrian
author
authority
  authorities
autoharp
automatic
  automatically
  automation
automobile
autonomy
  autonomous
autumn
  autumnal
auxiliary
  auxiliaries

av

avail
  available
  availability

average
  averaged
  averaging
avocation
avoid
  avoidable

aw

awake *(irreg. vb.)*
  awaken
  awaking
aware
  awareness
away *(gone)*
  [aweigh *(to clear anchor)*]
awesome
awful *(terrible)*
  [offal *(entrails)*]
  awfully
awl *(a tool)*
  [all *(everything)*]

ax

ax
  axes
axis
axle

ay

aye *(yes)*
  [eye *(used to see)*]
  [I *(myself)*]

ba

baby
  babied
  babies
back
background
backward
bacon
bacteria
  bacterial
bad
bag
  bagged
  bagger
  bagging
bail *(scoop out water)*
  [bale *(bundle)*]
bait *(lure)*
  [bate *(lessen)*]
bake
  baked
  baker
  baking
  bakery
  bakeries
balance
  balanced
  balancer
  balancing
bale *(bundle)*
  [bail *(scoop out water)*]
ball *(round object)*
  [bawl *(to cry)*]
ballet
ballgame
balloon
Baltimore
banana
band *(united group)*
  [banned *(forbidden)*]
bandage
  bandaged
  bandaging
bang
bank
banned *(forbidden)*
  [band *(united group)*]
bar
  barred *(shut out)*
  [bard *(a poet)*]
  barring

bard *(a poet)*
  [barred *(shut out)*]
bare *(nude)*
  [bear *(an animal)*]
  bared
  baring *(uncovering)*
  [bearing *(manner of acting)*]
bark
barn
barrel
base *(bottom of a structure)*
  [bass *(lowest voice)*]
  based
  bases *(more than one base)*
  [basis *(foundation)*]
  basing
baseball
basic
basin
basis *(foundation)*
  [bases *(more than one base)*]
basket
basketball
bass *(lowest voice)*
  [base *(bottom of a structure)*]
bat
  batted
  batter
  batting
bate *(lessen)*
  [bait *(lure)*]
bath
batter
battery
  batteries
battle
  battled
  battler
  battling
bawl *(to cry)*
  [ball *(round object)*]
bay

be

be *(exist)*
  [bee *(an insect)*]
beach *(shore)*
  [beech *(type of tree)*]
  beaches

bead
beam
bean
bear *(an animal)*
  [bare *(nude)*]
  bearing *(manner of acting)*
  [baring *(uncovering)*]
beast
beat *(hit) (irreg. vb.)*
  [beet *(type of vegetable)*]
  beating
beau *(boyfriend)*
  [bow *(decorative knot)*]
beauty
  beauties
  beautiful
beaver
became
because
become
  becoming
bed
  bedded
  bedding
bedroom

*The following regular endings are not in the word list and can be added to the root word without changes:
-ed, -er, -est, -ful, -ing, -less, -ly, -ness, and -s. Most exceptions and root changes are in the list.*

bee *(an insect)*
   [be *(exist)*]
beech *(type of tree)*
   [beach *(shore)*]
beef
been *(used to be)*
   [bin *(a container)*]
beep
beer *(a drink)*
   [bier *(a coffin)*]
beet *(type of vegetable)*
   [beat *(hit)*]
beetle
before
beg
   beggar
   begged
   begging
began
begin *(irreg. vb.)*
   beginning
begun
behalf
behave
   behaved
   behaving
behavior
   behavioral
behind
being
Belgium
belief
believe
   believable
   believed
   believer
   believing
bell *(something you ring)*
   [belle *(pretty girl)*]
belly
belong
below
belt
bench
   benches
bend *(irreg. vb.)*
beneath
benefit
bent
berry *(type of fruit)*
   [bury *(put in ground)*]
   berries
berth *(place to sleep)*
   [birth *(being born)*]

beside
best
bet *(irreg. vb.)*
   betting
   bettor
betray
better *(more good)*
   [bettor *(one who bets)*]
between
beyond

bi

Bible
bicycle
   bicycled
   bicycling
bid
bier *(coffin)*
   [beer *(a drink)*]
big
   bigger
   biggest
   bigness
bike
bill
   billed *(did bill)*
   [build *(construct)*]
billion
bin *(a container)*
   [been *(used to be)*]
biology
bird
birth *(being born)*
   [berth *(a place to sleep)*]
birthday
bit
bite *(irreg. vb.)*
   biting
bitter
bizarre

bl

blab
black
   blacken
   blackish
blade
blame
   blamed
   blaming
blank
blanket
blast

blaze
   blazed
   blazing
bled
bleed *(irreg. vb.)*
blend
blew *(did blow)*
   [blue *(a color)*]
blind
blink
block
blood
   bloodied
   bloodier
   bloodies
   bloodiest
   bloody
bloom
blossom
blouse
blow *(irreg. vb.)*
blue *(a color)*
   [blew *(did blow)*]
bluff

bo

boar *(pig)*
   [bore *(uninteresting)*]
board *(1. plank, 2. get on)*
   [bored *(uninterested)*]
   boarder *(one who boards)*
   [border *(boundary)*]
boat
body
   bodies
boil
bold
   bolder *(more bold)*
   [boulder *(big stone)*]

Bolivia
boll *(cotton pod)*
  [bowl *(1. a dish, 2 play tenpins)*]
bond
bone
  boned
  boning
bonnet
bonus
boo
book
bookkeeper
boom
boost
boot
border *(a boundary)*
  [boarder *(one who boards)*]
bore *(uninteresting)*
  [boar *(a pig)*]
  bored *(uninterested)*
  [board *(1. plank, 2. get on)*]
born *(delivered at birth)*
  [borne *(carried)*]
borne *(carried)*
  [born *(delivered at birth)*]
borough *(part of a city)*
  [burro *(donkey)*]
  [burrow *(to dig)*]
borrow
boss
  bossy
Boston
  Bostonian
both
bother
bottle
  bottled
  bottler
  bottling
bottom
bough *(limb of a tree)*
  [bow *(front end of a ship)*]
bought
bouillon *(clear broth)*
  [bullion *(uncoined gold or silver)*]
boulder *(a large rock)*
  [bolder *(more bold)*]
bounce

bound
boundary
  boundaries
bow *(decorating knot)*
  [beau *(boyfriend)*]
bow *(front end of a ship)*
  [bough *(limb of a tree)*]
bowl *(1. dish, 2. play tenpins)*
  [boll *(cotton pod)*]
box
  boxes
boy *(male child)*
  [buoy *(floating marker)*]

br

bracelet
brag
brain
  brainy
brake *(device for stopping vehicles)*
  [break *(take apart by forced)*]
  braked
  braking
branch
  branches
brand
brass
  brasses
  brassy
brave
  braved
  braver
  bravest
  braving
Brazil
  Brazilian
bread *(food)*
  [bred *(raised)*]
break *(take apart by force) (irreg. vb.)*
  [brake *(device for stopping vehicles)*]
breakfast
breath
breathe
  breathable
  breathed
  breather
  breathing

bred *(raised)*
  [bread *(a food)*]
breeze
  breezed
  breezing
brew
  brewed *(boiled)*
  [brood *(group of offspring)*]
  brews *(boils)*
  [bruise *(an injury)*]
brick
bridal *(relating to the bride)*
  [bridle *(part of a horse harness)*]
bridge
  bridged
  bridging
bridle *(part of a horse harness)*
  [bridal *(relating to a bride)*]
brief
bright
brilliant
bring *(irreg. vb.)*
  brought
Britain
  British
broad
broke
  broken
brood *(group of offspring)*
  [brewed *(boiled)*]
brook
brother
brought
brown
bruise *(an injury)*
  [brews *(boils)*]
brush
  brushes

The following regular endings are not in the word list and can be added to the root word without changes: -ed, -er, -est, -ful, -ing, -less, -ly, -ness, and -s. Most exceptions and root changes are in the list.

bu

bubble
  bubbled
  bubbling
  bubbly
buck
bucket
bud
  budded
  budding
buffalo
  buffaloes
bug
build *(construct) (irreg. vb.)*
  [billed *(did bill)*]
built
bulb
Bulgaria
bull
bullet
bullion *(uncoined gold or silver)*
  [bouillon *(clear broth)*]
bump
bunch
  bunches
bundle
  bundled
  bundling
buoy *(floating marker)*
  [boy *(male child)*]
burn
burro *(donkey)*
  [borough *(part of a city)*]
  [burrow *(to dig)*]
burrow *(see burro)*
burst *(irreg. vb.)*
bury *(put in ground)*
  [berry *(type of fruit)*]
bus
  buses
bush
  bushes
bushy
  bushier
  bushiest
  bushiness
business
  businesses
bust

busy
  busied
  busier
  busiest
  busily
but *(except)*
  [butt *(the hindmost end)*]
butter
  buttery
butterfly
  butterflies
button
buy *(purchase) (irreg. vb.)*
  [by *(beside)*]
  [bye *(farewell)*]

by

by *(beside)*
  [buy *(purchase)*]
  [bye *(farewell)*]
bye *(see by)*

ca

cabbage
cabin
cabinet
cache *(hiding place for goods)*
  [cash *(money)*]
cage
  caged
  caging
cake
  caked
  caking
calf
  calves
California
  Californian
call
callous *(unfeeling)*
  [callus *(hardened skin tissue)*]
callus *(see callous)*
calm
came
camel
camera
camp
campaign
can
    canned
    canner
    canning

Canada
  Canadian
canal
candle
candy
  candied
  candies
cane
cannon *(large military gun)*
  [canon *(law)*]
can't *(cannot)*
canvas *(sturdy cloth)*
  [canvass *(survey)*]
canyon
cap
  capped
  capping
capable
capacity
cape
capital *(1. money 2. seat of government)*
  [capitol *(a statehouse)*]
captain
capture
  captured
  capturing
car
carat *(jeweler's measure)*
  [caret *(proofreader's mark)*]
  [carrot *(a vegetable)*]
carbon
  carbonation
card
cardboard
care
  caring
career

caret *(proofreader's mark)*
  [carat *(jeweler's measure)*)]
  [carrot *(a vegetable)*)]
carol *(a song)*
  [carrel *(study space in a library)*)]
cargo
  cargoes
carpet
carrel *(study space in a library)*
  [carol *(a song)*)]
carriage
carrot *(a vegetable)*
  [carat *(jeweler's measure)*)]
  [caret *(proofreader's mark)*)]
carry
  carried
  carrier
  carries
cart
carve
  carved
  carver
  carving
case
  cased
  casing
cash *(money)*
  [cache *(hiding place for goods)*)]
  cashier
cast *(actors in a play)*
  [caste *(social class)*)]
castle
casual
cat
catch *(irreg. vb.)*
  catches
  caught *(did catch)*
caterpillar
cattle
Caucasian
caught
cause
  caused
  causing
caution
cave
  caved
  caving

ce

cede *(give over; surrender)*
  [seed *(part of a plant)*)]
ceiling *(top of a room)*
  [sealing *(closing)*)]
celebrate
  celebrant
  celebrated
  celebrating
  celebration
  celebrator
cell *(prison room)*
  [sell *(exchange for money)*)]
cellar *(basement)*
  [seller *(one who sells)*)]
cement
censor *(to ban)*
  [sensor *(detection device)*)]
cent *(a penny)*
  [scent *(odor)*)]
  [sent *(did send)*)]
  cents *(pennies)*
  [sense *(feel)*)]
center
central
century
  centuries
cereal *(food made from grain)*
  [serial *(of a series)*)]
ceremony
certain
  certainty
cession *(yielding)*
  [session *(a meeting)*)]

ch

chain
chair
chalk
challenge
  challenged
  challenger
  challenging
chamber
champion
  championship
chance
  chanced
  chancing

change
  changeable
  changed
  changing
channel
chapter
character
  characteristic
  characteristically
charge
  charged
  charging
charm
chart
chase
  chased *(did chase)*
  [chaste *(pure)*)]
  chaser
  chasing
chat
  chatter
  chatty
cheap *(inexpensive)*
  [cheep *(a bird sound)*)]
cheat
check
cheek
cheep *(a bird sound)*
  [cheap *(inexpensive)*)]
cheer
cheese
chemical
cherry
  cherries
chest
chic *(stylish)*
  [sheik *(Arab chief)*)]

The following regular endings are not in the word list and can be added to the root word without changes: -ed, -er, -est, -ful, -ing, -less, -ly, -ness, and -s. Most exceptions and root changes are in the list.

Chicago
  Chicagoan
chicken
chief
child
  children
Chile *(South American country)*
  [chili *(hot pepper)*]
  [chilly *(cold)*]
  Chilean
chili *(see Chile)*
chill
chilly *(see Chile)*
chimney
chin
China
  Chinese
chip
chocolate
choice
choir *(singing group)*
  [quire *(paper quantity)*]
choke
  choker
  choking
choose *(irreg. vb.)*
  choosey
  choosing
chop
choral *(of a choir)*
  [coral *(sea-animal skeleton)*]
chorale *(sacred hymn)*
  [corral *(pen for livestock)*]
chord *(group of musical notes)*
  [cord *(string)*]
chorus
  choruses
chose
  chosen
Christ
  Christian
chromosome
chronology
  chronological
  chronologies
chubby
chuckle
church
  churches
chute *(slide)*
  [shoot *(discharge gun)*]

ci

circle
  circled
  circling
circuit
circus
  circuses
cite *(give credit to a source)*
  [sight *(vision)*]
  [site *(location)*]
citizen
city
  cities
civil
  civilian
  civilization
  civilize
  civilized
  civilizing

cl

claim
  claimant
clam
clap
  clapped
  clapper
  clapping
clash
clasp
class
  classes
classify
  classification
  classifier
  classifies
classmate
classroom
clause *(part of a sentence)*
  [claws *(hooked nails on animals' feet)*]
claw
  claws *(hooked nails on animals' feet)*
  [clause *(part of a sentence)*]
clay
clean
clear
clerk
Cleveland
clever
click *(short, sharp sound)*
  [clique *(group of friends)*]

cliff
climate
climax
climb *(to ascend)*
  [clime *(climate)*]
cling
clip
clique *(group of friends)*
  [click *(short, sharp sound)*]
cloak
clock
close *(shut)*
  [clothes *(clothing)*]
  closed
  closes
  closing
close *(near)*
  closer
  closest
cloth
clothe
  clothed
  clothes *(clothing)*
  [close *(shut)*]
  clothing
cloud
club
clue *(hint, helps solve a mystery)*
  [clew *(a ball of yarn)*]

co

coach
  coaches
coal *(fuel)*
  [cole *(cabbage)*]
coarse *(rough)*
  [course *(1. path, 2. school subject)*]

coast
  coastal
coat
coax
  coaxes
code
  coded
  coder
  coding
coffee
coil
coin
cold
cole (*cabbage*)
  [coal (*fuel*)]
collage
collapse
  collapsed
  collapsing
collar
collect
  collection
  collector
college
  collegiate
collide
  collision
colonel (*military officer*)
  [kernel (*a seed or grain*)]
colony
  colonial
  colonies
  colonist
color
Colombia
Colorado
Columbus
column
coma (*unconsciousness*)
  [comma (*punctuation*)]
comb
combat
combine
  combination
  combined
  combining
come (*irreg. vb.*)
  coming
comedy
  comedies
comet

comfort
  comfortable
  comfortably
comic
  comical
comma (*punctuation*)
  [coma (*state of
  unconsciousness*)]
command
commence
  commenced
  commencing
commend
  commendable
  commendably
  commendation
comment
commerce
  commercial
  commercialism
commission
commit
  commitment
committee
common
commonplace
commotion
communicate
  communicated
  communicating
  communication
  communicator
Communism
  Communist
community
  communities
compact
companion
company
  companies
compare
  compared
  comparing
  comparison
compass
  compasses
compatible
compel
compensate
  compensated
  compensating

compete
competent
competition
complain
complement (*completing part*)
  [compliment (*praise*)]
  complementary
  (*completes*)
  [complimentary (*free*)]
complete
  completed
  completing
complex
  complexes
  complexion
complicate
  complicated
  complication
compliment (*praise*)
  [complement (*completing
  part*)]
  complimentary (*free*)
  [complementary
  (*completes*)]
component
compose
  composed
  composer
  composing
composite
  composition
compound
comprehend
  comprehension
compress
  compression
  compressor
compromise
compute
  computation
  computed
computer
  computing

The following regular endings are not in the word list and can be added to the root word without changes:
-ed, -er, -est, -ful, -ing, -less, -ly, -ness, and -s. Most exceptions and root changes are in the list.

comrade
concave
conceal
conceive
  conceived
concentrate
  concentrated
  concentrating
  concentration
concept
  conception
  conceptual
concern
concert
concession
conclude
  conclusion
concrete
condemn
  condemnation
condense
  condensed
condition
conduct
  conductor
cone
conference
confess
  confession
confide
  confident
  confidential
confine
  confined
  confining
confirm
conflict
conform
confront
  confrontation
confuse
  confused
  confusing
  confusion
congress
  congresses
  congressional
congruent
conjunction
connect
  connection
  connector
Connecticut

connotation
conquer
  conqueror
conscience *(noun)*
  conscious *(adjective)*
consecutive
consent
consequence
conserve
  conservation
consider
  considerable
  considerably
  considerate
consist
  consistence
  consistency
  consistent
consonant
constant
constitution
  constitutional
construct
  construction
consult
  consultation
consume
  consumed
  consumer
  consuming
  consumption
contact
contagious *(easily spread)*
  contiguous *(touching)*
contain
content
contest
  contestant
continent
  continental
continue
  continual *(no interruption, again and again)*
  continually
  continued
  continuing
  continuous *(uninterrupted, unbroken)*
contract
contraction
contrary
contrast

contribute
  contributed
  contributing
  contribution
  contributor
control
  controllable
  controlled
  controller
  controlling
controversy
  controversial
convenient
  convenience
convention
  conventional
conversation
  conversational
converse
convert
  convertible
convex
convict
  conviction
convince
  convinced
  convincing
cook
cookie
cool
coop *(chicken pen)*
  [coupe *(type of car)*]
copper
copy
  copied
  copier
  copies
coral *(sea-animal skeleton)*
  [choral *(of a choir)*]

cord *(string)*
  [chord *(group of musical notes)*]
  cordless
core *(the center)*
  [corps *(group of military personnel)*]
  cored
  coring
corn
corps *(group of military personnel)*
  [core *(the center)*]
corner
corral *(pen for livestock)*
  [chorale *(sacred hymn)*]
correct
  correction
correspond
  correspondence
  correspondent
corrupt
cosmic
cost *(irreg. vb.)*
Costa Rica
costume
  costumed
  costuming
cottage
cotton
couch
cough
could
couldn't *(could not)*
council *(legislative body)*
  [counsel *(to advise)*]
counsel *(to advise)*
  [council *(legislative body)*]
  counselor
count
country
  countries
county
  counties
coupe *(type of car)*
  [coop *(chicken pen)*]

couple
  coupled
  coupling
courage
  courageous
course *(1. path, 2. school subject)*
  [coarse *(rough)*]
  coursed
  coursing
court
cousin
cover
cow
coward
cowboy

cr

crack
craft
  crafty
crash
  crashes
crawl
crayon
crazy
  crazier
  craziest
  crazily
creak *(squeaking sound)*
  [creek *(a stream)*]
cream
  creamy
create
  created
  creating
  creation
  creative
  creator
creature
credible
credit
  creditor
credulous
creek *(a stream)*
  [creak *(squeaking sound)*]
creep *(irreg. vb.)*
  crept *(did creep)*

crew
  crews *(groups of workers)*
  [cruise *(an ocean voyage)*]
crib
crocodile
crop
  cropped
  cropping
cross
crow
crowd
crown
cruel
cruise *(an ocean voyage)*
  [crews *(groups of workers)*]
crush
  crushes
crust
cry
  cried
  crier
  cries
crystal

cu

cub
Cuba
  Cuban
cube
  cubed
  cubing
cue *(to prompt)*
  [queue *(line of people)*]
culture
  cultural
  cultured
  culturist
cup
  cupped
  cupping
curious
  curiosity
curl

The following regular endings are not in the word list and can be added to the root word without changes: -ed, -er, -est, -ful, -ing, -less, -ly, -ness, and -s. Most exceptions and root changes are in the list.

currant *(small raisin)*
  [current *(1. recent, 2. fast-flowing part of a stream)*]
current *(see currant)*
curser *(one who curses)*
  [cursor *(moving pointer on computer screen)*]
curtain
curvature
curve
  curved
  curving
cushion
custom
cut
  cutting

cy
cycle
  cycled
  cycling
  cyclist
cyclone
cylinder
  cylindrical
cymbal *(a percussion instrument)*
  [symbol *(a sign)*]

cz
Czechoslovakia

da
dad
daily
dairy
  dairies
Dallas
dam *(stop flow)*
  [damn *(curse)*]
  dammed
  damming
damage
  damaged
  damages
  damaging
damp
dance
  danced
  dancer
  dancing

danger
  dangerous
dare
  dared
  daring
dark
  darken
dash
date
  dated
  dating
datum
  data
daughter
dawn
day
  days *(parts of a week)*
  [daze *(to stun and confuse)*]
daze *(to stun and confuse)*
  [days *(parts of a week)*]

de
dead
deaf
deal
  dealt
dear *(much loved)*
  [deer *(type of animal)*]
death
decease
December
decide
  decided
  deciding
decimal
decision
deck
declare
  declaration
  declared
  declaring
deep
  deepen
deer *(type of animal)*
  [dear *(much loved)*]
defeat
defect
defense
  defensible
  defensive
define
  defined
  defining

definite
  definition
degree
Delaware
delay
delicate
delicious
delight
delinquent
  delinquencies
  delinquency
deliver
  deliverance
  deliveries
  delivery
demand
Denmark
  Danish
denominator
dense
  denser
  densities
  density
Denver
deny
  denial
  denied
depart
department
depend
  dependable
  dependence
  dependency
  dependent
deposit
  depositor
depth
deputy
derive
  derived
  deriving

describe
  described
  describing
  description
desert *(leave)*
  [dessert *(pie)*]
  desertion
design
designate
  designated
  designating
  designation
desire
  desirable
  desired
  desiring
desk
despite
despot
dessert *(pie)*
  [desert *(leave)*]
destroy
destruction
detail
determine
  determined
  determining
Detroit
develop
  development
  developmental
device
devil
  deviltry
dew *(water droplets)*
  [do *(perform)*]
  [due *(payable)*]

di

diagnosis
diagonal
diagram
  diagrammed
  diagramming
dial
diameter
diamond
dictionary
  dictionaries
did
didn't *(did not)*

die *(stop living)*
  [dye *(to color)*]
  died
  dying
diet
  dietitian
differ
  difference
  different
  differentiate
difficult
  difficulties
  difficulty
dig *(irreg. vb.)*
  digger
  digging
digit
  digital
dim
  dimmed
  dimmer
  dimmest
dime
dimension
  dimensional
dine
  dined
  diner
  dining
dinner
dinosaur
dip
direct
  direction
  director
dirt
  dirtier
  dirtiest
  dirty
disable
disagree
  disagreeable
  disagreement
disappear
  disappearance
disappoint
disapprove
disaster
disburse *(pay out)*
  [disperse *(scatter)*]
discomfort
discourage

discover
  discovery
  discoveries
discreet *(wisely cautious)*
  [discrete *(separate)*]
discrepancy
  discrepancies
discriminate
discuss
  discusses
  discussion
disease
disguise
dish
  dishes
disinterested *(impartial or without prejudice)*
  [uninterested *(indifferent or without interest)*]
dislike
disperse *(scatter)*
  [disburse *(pay out)*]
display
dispute
disrupt
dissolve
  dissolved
  dissolving
distant
  distance
distinguish
  distinguishable
  distinguishes
dive *(irreg. vb.)*
  diver
  diving
diverge
  diverged
  diverging

The following regular endings are not in the word list and can be added to the root word without changes: -ed, -er, -est, -ful, -ing, -less, -ly, -ness, and -s. Most exceptions and root words changes are in the list.

diverse
  diversify
divide
  divided
  dividing
  divisibility
  divisible
  division
divulge
  divulged
  divulging

do

do *(perform) (irreg. vb.)*
  [dew *(water droplets)*]
  [due *(payable)*]
dock
doctor
doe *(female deer)*
  [dough *(bread mixture)*]
does
doesn't *(does not)*
dog
doll
dollar
done *(finished)*
  [dun *(1. demand payment,*
  2. dull color)]
donkey
don't *(do not)*
door
doorway
dot
  dotted
  dotting
double
  doubled
  doubling
doubt
dough *(bread mixture)*
  [doe *(female deer)*]
dove
down
  downed
downward
dozen

dr

drag
  dragged
  dragging
dragon
dramatic
  dramatically

drank
draw *(irreg. vb.)*
drawer
dream *(irreg. vb.)*
  dreamy
dress
  dresses
drew
drift
drill
  drilled
  driller
  drilling
drink *(irreg. vb.)*
drive *(irreg. vb.)*
  driver
  driving
drop
  dropped
  dropper
  dropping
drove
drown
drug
  drugged
drum
  drummed
  drummer
  drumming
drunk
dry
  dried
  drier
  dries
  driest

du

dual *(two)*
  [duel *(formal combat)*]
duck
  ducked *(did duck)*
  [duct *(tube or pipe)*]
due *(payable)*
  [dew *(water droplets)*]
  [do *(perform)*]
duel *(formal combat)*
  [dual *(two)*]
dug
duke
dull
  dully
dumb
dump

dun *(1. demand payment, 2.*
  dull color)
  [done *(finished)*]
during
dust
Dutch
duty
  duties

dy

dye *(color)*
  [die *(stop living)*]
  dyed

ea

each
eager
eagle
ear
early
  earlier
  earliest
earn *(work for)*
  [urn *(vase)*]
earth
earthquake
ease
  eased
  easing
east *(direction)*
  eastern
East *(geographical area)*
easy
  easier
  easiest
  easily
eat *(irreg. vb.)*

eb
ebb
ebony

ec
echo
   echoes
economy
   economic
   economies
Ecuador

ed
edge
   edged
   edger
   edging
educate
   education

ee
eerie
   eerier
   eerily
   eeriness

ef
effect *(the result)*
   [affect *(to influence)*]
   effective
efficient
   efficiency
effort

eg
egg
Egypt
   Egyptian

ei
eight *(the number 8)*
   [ate *(did eat)*]
   eighth
eighteen
   eighteenth
eighty
   eighties
   eightieth
either

el
elect
   election
   elector
electric
   electrical
   electrician
   electricity
electron
   electronic
element
elephant
elevate
   elevated
   elevating
   elevation
   elevator
eleven
   eleventh
else

em
emigrate *(leave your country)*
   [immigrate *(to come to a
   country to live)*]
   emigrated
   emigrating
   emigration
eminent *(famous, outstanding)*
   [imminent *(may occur at
   any moment)*]
emotional
emperor
empire
employ
   employable
empty
   emptied
   emptier
   empties
   emptiness

en
enable
   enabled
   enabling
enclose
   enclosure

encourage
   encouraged
   encouraging
encyclopedia
end
enemy
   enemies
energy
   energies
enforce
engage
   engaged
   engaging
engine
   engineer
England
   English
enjoy
   enjoyable
enormous
enough
ensure *(make certain)*
   [insure *(buy or sell
   insurance)*]
   ensured
   ensuring
enter
entertain
entire
entrance
entry
   entries
environment
   environmental

The following regular endings are not in the word list and can be added to the root word without changes:
-ed, -er, -est, -ful, -ing, -less, -ly, -ness, and -s. Most exceptions and root changes are in the list.

eq

equal
  equality
equation
equator
equip
  equipped
  equipping
equipment
equivalent

er

erase
  eraser
  erasing
error
  erroneous
erupt
  eruption

es

escape
  escaped
  escaping
Eskimo
especial
essential
establish
  establishes
estimate
  estimated
  estimating
  estimation
  estimator

eu

Europe
  European

ev

even
evening
event
eventual
ever
every
everybody
everyday
everyone
everything
everywhere

evidence
  evidenced
evil

ew

ewe *(female sheep)*
  [yew *(a shrub)*]
  [you *(yourself)*]

ex

exact
examination
examine
  examined
  examiner
  examining
example
except *(to exclude)*
  [accept *(to receive)*]
  exception
excerpt
exchange
  exchanged
  exchanging
excite
  excited
  exciting
  excitement
exclaim
exclude
excuse
  excused
  excusing
exercise
  exercised
  exercising
exert
  exertion
exhibit
  exhibition
  exhibitor
exhausted
  exhausting
  exhaustion
exist
  existence
exit
expander
  expansion
expect
  expectation
expedition
expense
  expensive

experience
  experienced
  experiencing
experiment
  experimental
expert
explain
  explanation
explode
explore
  exploration
  explored
  explorer
  exploring
express
  expresses
  expression
extend
extra
extraordinary
extreme

ey

eye *(used to see)*
  [aye *(yes)*]
  [I *(myself)*]
  eyed
eyelet *(small hole)*
  [islet *(small island)*]

fa

fable
fabric
fabulous
face
  faced
  facing
fact
  factual

factory
   factories
factor
fail
faint *(weak)*
   [feint *(false attack)*]
fair *(1. honest, 2. a bazaar)*
   [fare *(cost of ticket)*]
fairy *(an imaginary being)*
   [ferry *(a river-crossing boat)*]
   fairies
faith
fall *(irreg. vb.)*
   fallen
fallible
false
familiar
family
   families
fan
   fanned
   fanning
fancy
   fancied
   fancier
   fancies
   fanciest
fantastic
far
fare *(cost of ticket)*
   [fair *(1. honest, 2. a bazaar)*]
farm
farther *(physical distance)*
   [further *(greater extent)*]
fascinate
   fascination
fashion
   fashionable
fast
   fasten
fat
   fatter
   fattest
father
fault
favor
   favorable
   favorite
faze *(upset)*
   [phase *(a stage)*]

fe

fear
feast
feat *(accomplishment)*
   [feet *(plural of foot)*]
feather
feature
   featured
   featuring
February
fed
federal
feed *(irreg. vb.)*
feel
feet *(plural of foot)*
   [feat *(accomplishment)*]
feint *(false attach)*
   [faint *(weak)*]
fell
fellow
felt
female
fence
   fenced
   fencing
ferry *(a river-crossing boat)*
   [fairy *(an imaginary being)*]
fertile
   fertility
festival
festive
fever
few

fi

fiber
field
fierce
   fiercer
   fiercest
fifteen
   fifteenth
fifth
fifty
   fifties
   fiftieth
fig
fight
figure

figured
   figuring
file
   filed
   filing
fill
film
final
find *(discover) (irreg. vb.)*
   [fined *(forced to pay money as punishment)*]
fine
   fined *(forced to pay money as punishment)*
   [find *(discover)*]
   finer
   finest
   fining
finger
finish
   finishes
Finland
   Finish
fir *(type of tree)*
   [fur *(animal covering)*]
fire
   fired
   firing

The following regular endings are not in the word list and can be added the root word without changes:
-ed, -er, -est, -ful, -ing, -less, -ly, -ness, and -s. Most exceptions and root changes are in the list.

fireplace
firm
first
fish
    fishes
fisherman
    fishermen
fist
fit
    fitted
    fitting
five
    fifth
fix
    fixed
    fixes

fl

flag
    flagged
    flagging
flair *(natural talent)*
    [flare *(flaming signal)*]
flammable
    flammability
flame
    flamed
    flaming
flap
flare *(flaming signal)*
    [flair *(natural talent)*]
flash
    flashes
flat
    flatten
flaunt
flavor
flea *(insect)*
    [flee *(run away) (irreg. vb.)*]
flee *(see flea)*
fleet
flew *(did fly)*
    [flu *(influenza)*]
    [flue *(chimney part)*]
flight
flip
float
flood
floor
floral
Florida
flotation
flour *(milled grain)*
    [flower *(blossom)*]

flow
flower *(blossom)*
    [flour *(milled grain)*]
flu *(influenza)*
    [flew *(did fly)*]
    [flue *(chimney part)*]
flute
    fluted
    fluting
fly *(irreg. vb.)*
    flies

fo

fog
    fogging
    foggy
fold
folk
follow
food
fool
    foolish
foot
football
for *(in favor of)*
    [fore *(front part)*]
    [four *(the number 4)*]
forbade
forbid *(irreg. vb.)*
force
    forced
    forcing
ford
fore *(front part)*
    [for *(in favor of)*]
    [four *(the number 4)*]
forehead
foreign
forest
forever
foreword *(a preface)*
    [forward *(toward the front)*]
forgave
forget
    forgettable
    forgetting
forgot
    forgotten
fork
form
formal
    formally *(properly)*
    [formerly *(before now)*]

formation
former
    formerly *(before now)*
    [formally *(properly)*]
formula
fort
forth *(forward)*
    [fourth *(after third)*]
fortune
    fortunate
forty
    forties
    fortieth
forward *(toward the front)*
    [foreword *(a preface)*]
fossil
fought
foul *(bad)*
    [fowl *(a bird)*]
found
four *(the number 4)*
    [for *(in favor of)*]
    [fore *(front part)*]
    fourth *(after third)*
    [forth *(forward)*]
fourteen
    fourteenth
fowl *(a bird)*
    [foul *(bad)*]
fox
    foxes

fr

fraction
  fractional
frame
  framed
  framing
franc *(French money)*
  [frank *(honest)*]
France
  French
frank *(honest)*
  [franc *(French money)*]
free
  freed
  freer
  freest
freedom
freeze *(irreg. vb.)*
  freezing
French
frequent
  frequencies
  frequency
fresh
  freshen
friar *(member of religious order)*
  [fryer *(frying chicken)*]
Friday
friend
  friendlier
  friendliest
  friendly
fright
  frighten
frog
from
front
  frontier
frost
froze
  frozen
fruit
fry
  fried
  fryer *(frying chicken)*
  [friar *(member of religious order)*]

fu

fuel
full
fun
function
funny
  funnier
  funniest
fur *(animal covering)*
  [fir *(type of tree)*]
furnace
furniture
further *(greater extent)*
  [farther *(physical distance)*]
future

ga

gain
gaiety
gait *(pace)*
  [gate *(fence)*]
gallon
game
gang
garage
garden
garment
gas
  gases
gasoline
gate *(fence)*
  [gait *(pace)*]
gather
gauge
  gauged
  gauges
gave
gay

ge

gear
gene
general
generation
generous
genius

gentle
  gentled
  gentler
  gentlest
  gently
gentleman
  gentlemen
geography
  geographies
geology
geometry
  geometric
  geometrically
Georgia
germ
Germany
  German
get *(irreg. vb.)*
  getting

gh

ghastly
ghetto
ghost
ghoul

gi

giant
gift
gilt *(golden)*
  [guilt *(opposite of innocence)*]
girl
give *(irreg. vb.)*
  giver
  giving

The following regular endings are not in the word list and can be added to the root word without changes: -ed, -er, -est, -ful, -ing, -less, -ly, -ness, and -s. Most exceptions and root changes are in the list.

gl

glacial
glacier
glad
    gladder
    gladdest
glance
    glanced
    glancing
glass
    glasses
    glassy
glee
glimpse
glint
globe
    global
glory
    glories
    glorious
glow
glue
    glued
    gluing

gn

gnu *(African antelope)*
    [knew *(did know)*]
    [new *(opposite of old)*]

go

go *(irreg. vb.)*
    goes
goal
goat
god
gold
    golden
gone
good
good-bye
goose
gorilla *(type of ape)*
    [guerrilla *(irregular soldier)*]
got
government
    governmental
governor

gr

grab
    grabbed
    grabbing
grace
grade
    graded
    grading
gradual
grain
grammar
grand
grandfather
grandmother
grant
grape
graph
grass
    grasses
grassland
grate *(to grind)*
    [great *(1. large, 2. excellent)*]
grave
gravity
    gravities
gray
graze
    grazed
    grazing
great *(1. large, 2. excellent)*
    [grate *(to grind)*]
Great Britain
Greece
    Greek
greed
green
greet
grew
grief
grieve
    grievance
    grieved
    grieving
grin
    grinned
    grinning
grind *(irreg. vb.)*
grip
groan *(moan)*
    [grown *(mature; adult)*]
grocery
    groceries

ground
group
grow *(irreg. vb.)*
    grown *(mature; adult)*
    [groan *(moan)*]
    growth

gu

guard
Guatemala
guerilla *(irregular soldier)*
    [gorilla *(type of ape)*]
guess
guest *(visitor)*
    [guessed *(surmised)*]
guide
    guidance
    guided
    guiding
guilt *(opposite of innocence)*
    [gilt *(golden)*]
guitar
    guitarist
gulf
gum
gun
    gunned
    gunner
    gunning
guy

ha

habit
  habitual
habitat
had
hadn't *(had not)*
hail *(frozen rain)*
  [hale *(healthy)*]
hair *(growth on head)*
  [hare *(type of rabbit)*]
Haiti
  Haitian
hale *(healthy)*
  [hail *(frozen rain)*]
half
halfway
hall *(passage between rooms)*
  [haul *(to carry)*]
halve *(to cut in half)*
  [have *(possess)*]
hammer
hand
handicap
handle
  handled
  handling
handsome
  handsomer
  handsomest
handwriting
hang
hangar *(storage building)*
  [hanger *(tool for draping clothing)*]
happen
happy
  happier
  happiest
  happily
  happiness
harass
  harassment
harbor
hard
  hardier
  hardily
  hardy
hare *(type of rabbit)*
  [hair *(growth on head)*]
harm

harmony
  harmonious
harness
  harnesses
harsh
harvest
has
hat
  hatter
hatch
  hatches
hate
  hated
  hating
haul *(to carry)*
  [hall *(passage between rooms)*]
have *(possess)*
  [halve *(cut in half)*]
  having
haven't *(have not)*
Hawaii
  Hawaiian
hawk
hay *(dried grass)*
  [hey *(expression to get someone's attention)*]

he

he
head
heal *(make well)*
  [heel *(back part of foot)*]
  [he'll *(he will)*]
health
  healthier
  healthiest
  healthily
  healthy
hear *(listen) (irreg. vb.)*
  [here *(this place)*]
  heard *(listened)*
  [herd *(group of animals)*]
heart
heat
heaven
heavy
  heavier
  heaviest
  heavily
  heaviness

he'd *(he would)*
  [heed *(pay attention to)*]
heel *(back part of foot)*
  [heal *(make well)*]
  [he'll *(he will)*]
height
heir *(successor)*
  [air *(what you breathe)*]
held
helicopter
he'll *(he will)*
  [heal *(make well)*]
  [heel *(back part of foot)*]
hello
helmet
help
hemisphere
hen
her
herd *(group of animals)*
  [heard *(listened)*]
here *(this place)*
  [hear *(listen)*]
hero
  heroes
  heroic
  heroine
herself
hew *(chop)*
  [hue *(a shade or color)*]
hey *(expression to get someone's attention)*
  [hay *(dried grass)*]

The following regular endings are not in the word list and can be added to the root word without changes: -ed, -er, -est, -ful, -ing, -less, -ly, -ness, and -s. Most exceptions and root changes are in the list.

hi

hi *(word of getting)*
  [high *(elevated)*]
hid
  hidden
hide *(irreg. vb.)*
  hiding
high *(elevated)*
  [hi *(word of greeting)*]
highland
highway
hill
him *(that man or boy)*
  [hymn *(religious song)*]
himself
hip
hire *(employ)*
  [higher *(above)*]
his
Hispanic
history
  histories
hit
  hitter
  hitting

ho

hoard *(hidden supply)*
  [horde *(a crowd)*]
hoarse *(sounding rough and
  deep)*
  [horse *(type of animal)*]
hog
hold *(irreg. vb.)*
hole *(an opening)*
  [whole *(complete)*]
  holey *(full of holes)*
  [holy *(sacred)*]
  [wholly *(completely)*]
home
  homey
  homeward
homonym
Honduras
honest
  honesty
Honolulu
honor
  honorable
hook
hop
  hopped
  hopping

hope
  hoped
  hoping
horde *(a crowd)*
  [hoard *(hidden supply)*]
horizon
  horizontal
horn
horse *(type of animal)*
  [hoarse *(sounding rough
  and deep)*]
hospitable
  hospitality
hospital
  hospitalize
hostel *(inn for young travelers)*
  [hostile *(unfriendly)*]
hot
  hotter
  hottest
hotel
hour *(60-minute period)*
  [our *(belonging to us)*]
house
  housed
  housing
Houston
how
however
howl

hu

hue *(a shade or color)*
  [hew *(chop)*]
huge
human
  humanism
  humanitarian
  humanity
  humanize
  humankind
  humanoid
humor
hump
hundred
hung
Hungary
  Hungarian
hunger
hungry
  hungrier
  hungriest
  hungrily
hunt

hurry
  hurried
  hurriedly
hurt

hy

hydrogen
hymn *(religious song)*
  [him *(that man or boy)*]
hypocrite

i

I *(myself)*
  [aye *(yes)*]
  [eye *(used to see)*]

ic

ice
  iced
  icily
icing
Iceland
icicle

id

I'd *(I would)*
Idaho
idea

ideal
identify
  identifies
identity
  identities
idle *(lazy)*
  [idol *(object of worship)*]
idol *(see idle)*

if
if

ig
ignite
  ignited
  igniting
ignition
ignore
  ignorance
  ignorant

il
ill
I'll *(I will)*
  [aisle *(narrow path)*]
  [isle *(island)*]
Illinois
illuminate
  illuminated
  illuminating
illustration

im
I'm *(I am)*
image
imagery
imagine
  imaginable
  imaginary
  imagination
  imagined
  imagining
immediate
  immediacy
immigrate *(to come to a country to live)*
  [emigrate *(leave your country)*]
  immigrant
  immigrated
  immigrating

imminent *(may occur at any moment)*
  [eminent *(famous, outstanding)*]
imply
  implied
  implies
important
  importance
impossible
  impossibility
  impossibly
impostor
impression
improve
  improved
  improving

in
in *(opposite of out)*
  [inn *(type of hotel)*]
inch
include
  included
  including
  inclusion
income
increase
  increased
  increasing
incredible
indeed
independent
  independence
index
India
  Indian
Indiana
Indianapolis
indicate
  indicated
  indicating
  indication
  indicative
individual
industry
  industrial
  industries
inert
  inertia

inevitable
  inevitability
  inevitably
infer
  inference
influence
  influenced
  influencing
  influential
influenza
information
  informative
initial
ink
inland
inn *(type of hotel)*
  [in *(opposite of out)*]
inner
innocent
insect
insert
inside
insist
  insistence
instance *(an example or a situation)*
  [instants *(very short periods of time)*]
instant
instead
instinct
instruct
  instruction
  instructive
  instructor

The following regular endings are not in the word and can be added to the root word without changes: -ed, -er, -est, -ful, -ing, -less, -ly, -ness, and -s. Most exceptions and root changes are in the list.

instrument
  instrumental
  instrumentation
insure *(buy or sell insurance)*
  [ensure *(make certain)*]
  insurance
  insured
  insuring
intend
intense *(extreme)*
  [intents *(purposes)*]
  intensify
  intensity
  intensive
  intention
  intentional
interest
interior
internal
international
interrupt
intersect
  intersected
  intersecting
  intersection
interval
interview
into
introduce
  introduced
  introducing
  introduction
invent
  invention
  inventor
investigate
  investigated
  investigating
  investigation
  investigative
  investigator
invisible
  invisibility
  invisibly
invite
  invitation
  invited
  inviting
involve
  involved
  involvement
  involving
invulnerable
Iowa

ir
Iran
  Iranian
Iraq
  Iraqi
irate
Ireland
  Irish
iris
iron
irony
  ironic
  ironically

is
is *(irreg. vb.)*
island
isle *(island)*
  [aisle *(narrow path)*]
  [I'll *(I will)*]
islet *(small island)*
  [eyelet *(small hole)*]
isn't *(is not)*
Israel
  Israeli
issue
  issued
  issuing

it
it
italic
it's *(it is)*
its *(belong to it)*
Italy
  Italian
item
  itemize
itself

ja
jacket
Jacksonville
jail
  jailor
jam *(fruit jelly)*
  [jamb *(part of a door frame)*]
jamb *(see jam)*
January
Japan
  Japanese

jar
  jarred
  jarring
jaw
jazz
  jazzier
  jazziest
  jazzy

je
jest
  jester
jet
  jetted
  jetting
  jettison
jetty
  jetties
jewel

ji
jiggle
jigsaw
jingle
  jingled
  jingling
jinx
  jinxes

jo
job
jobholder
jobless
join
joint

joke
  joked
  joker
  joking
journal
journey
journeyman
joy

ju

judge
  judged
  judgement
  judging
juice
July
jump
June
jungle
junior
jury
just
justice
justify
  justifiable
  justification

ka

Kansas

ke

keep *(irreg. vb.)*
kelp
Kentucky
kept
kernel *(a seed or grain)*
  [colonel *(military officer)*]
kettle
key
keyhole
keynote
keypunch
keystone

ki

kick
kid
  kidded
  kidding
kill

kind
kindle
  kindled
  kindling
king
kingdom
kink
kitchen
kite
kitten

kn

knead *(mix with hands)*
  [need *(require)*]
knee
kneel *(irreg. vb.)*
knew *(did know)*
  [gnu *(African antelope)*]
  [new *(opposite of old)*]
knife
  knives
knight *(servant of a king)*
  [night *(evening)*]
knit *(weave with yarn)*
  [nit *(louse egg)*]
knock
knot *(tangle)*
  [not *(negative)*]
  knotty *(full of tangles)*
  [naughty *(bad)*]
knothole
know *(familiar with) (irreg. vb.)*
  [no *(expression of refusal)*]
knowledge
  knowledgeable
  knowledgeably
known

ko

Korea

la

label
labor
laboratory
  laboratories
lack
lad
ladder

lady
  ladies
laid
lain *(past participle of lie)*
  [lane *(narrow street or path)*]
lake
lam *(to leave quickly)*
  lamb *(baby sheep)*
lamb *(see lam)*
land
landscape
lane *(narrow street or path)*
  [lain *(past participle of lie)*]
language
lap
  lapped
  lapping
large
  larger
  largest
last
late
  later
  latest
Latin
latitude
  latitudinal

The following regular endings are not in the word list and can be added to the root word without changes: -ed, -er, -est, -ful, -ing, -less, -ly, -ness, and -s. Most exceptions and root changes are in the list.

latter
laugh
   laughable
   laughter
law
lawn
lay *(past tense of lie) (irreg. vb.)*
   [lei *(flower necklace)*]
layer
lazy
   lazier
   laziest
   lazily
   laziness

le

lead *(a metal)*
   [led *(guided)*]
lead *(to guide) (irreg. vb.)*
leaf
   leaves
league
leak *(to drip)*
   [leek *(a vegetable)*]
lean *(1. slender, 2. slant to the side)*
   [lien *(a legal claim)*]
leap *(irreg. vb.)*
learn
lease
   leased *(rented)*
   [least *(smallest)*]
least *(smallest)*
   [leased *(rented)*]
leather
leave
   leaving
led *(guided)*
   [lead *(a metal)*]
leek *(a vegetable)*
   [leak *(to drip)*]
left
leg
legal
   legality
   legalize
legend
   legendary
leg
lei *(flower necklace)*
   [lay *(past tense of lie)*]
leisure
lend *(irreg. vb.)*
length

lens
   lenses
less
   lessen *(make less)*
   [lesson *(instruction)*]
   lesser *(of less size)*
   [lessor *(one who rents property)*]
lesson *(instruction)*
   [lessen *(make less)*]
lessor *(one who rents property)*
   [lesser *(of less size)*]
let
   letting
let's *(let us)*
levee *(an embankment)*
   [levy *(impose a tax)*]
level
lever
levy *(impose a tax)*
   [levee *(an embankment)*]

li

liable
liar
liberal
   liberalism
   liberalize
liberate
liberation
Liberia
   Liberian
liberty
   liberties
library
   libraries
license
lichen *(fungus)*
   [liken *(compare)*]
lick
lid
lie *(1. falsify, 2. recline) (irreg. vb.)*
   [lye *(alkaline solution)*]
   lying
lien *(a legal claim)*
   [lean *(1. slender, 2. slant to the side)*]
lieu *(instead of)*
   [Lou *(a name)*]
life
lifelike
lifeline
lifetime

lifework
lift
light *(irreg. vb.)*
lightning
like
   liked
   liken *(compare)*
   [lichen *(fungus)*]
   liking
limb
limit
   limitation
line
   lined
   lining
link
   linkage
lion
lip
liquid
liquor
list
listen
literacy
   literate
literal
literature
little
   littler
   littlest

live
  lived
  livelier
  liveliest
  liveliness
  lively
  living
lizard

lo

load *(burden)*
  [lode *(vein of ore)*]
loaf
  loaves
loan *(something borrowed)*
  [lone *(single)*]
loathe
local
locate
  located
  locating
  location
lock
lode *(vein of ore)*
  [load *(burden)*]
log
  logged
  logger
  logging
logic
  logical
London
  Londoner
lone *(single)*
  [loan *(something
  borrowed)*]
  lonelier
  loneliest
long
longitude
look
loop
loose *(not fastened or
  restrained)*
  [lose *(to come to be
  without)*]
  looser
  loosest
loot *(steal)*
  [lute *(stringed musical
  instrument)*]
lord

Los Angeles
lose *(to come to be without)*
  (irreg. vb.)
  [loose *(not fastened or
  restrained)*]
  loser
  losing
loss
  losses
lost
lot
Lou *(a name)*
  [lieu *(instead of)*]
Louisiana
loud
love
  loved
  lovelier
  loveliest
  loveliness
  lovely
  lover
  loving
low
lowland

lu

luck
  luckier
  luckiest
  luckily
  lucky
lumber
lump
lunch
  lunches
lung
lute *(stringed musical
  instrument)*
  [loot *(steal)*]
Luxembourg

ly

lye *(alkaline solution)*
  [lie *(1. falsify, 2. recline)*]

ma

ma
machine
  machined

mad
  madder
  maddest
made *(manufactured)*
  [maid *(domestic servant)*]
magazine
magic
magnate *(person of power)*
  [magnet *(metal that
  attracts other metals)*]
magnet *(metal that attracts
  other metals)*
  [magnate *(person of
  power)*]
  magnetic
maid *(domestic servant)*
  [made *(manufactured)*]
mail *(send by post)*
  [male *(man or boy)*]
main *(most important)*
  [Maine *(a state)*]
  [mane *(horse's neck hair)*]
Maine *(see main)*
maintain
  maintenance
maize *(Indian corn)*
  [maze *(confusing network
  of paths)*]

*The following regular endings are not in the word list and can be added to the root word without changes:
-ed, -er, -est, -ful, -ing, -less, -ly, -ness, and -s. Most exceptions and root changes are in the list.*

major
majority
  majorities
make
  maker
  making
male *(man or boy)*
  [mail *(send by post)*]
mall *(courtyard)*
  [maul *(mangle)*]
mama
mammal
  mammalian
man
  manned
  manning
  men
manage
  manageable
  managed
  management
  manager
  managing
mane *(horse's neck hair)*
  [main *(most important)*]
  [Maine *(a state)*]
manner *(way of behaving)*
  [manor *(mansion)*]
mantel *(shelf over fireplace)*
  [mantle *(cloak)*]
mantle *(see mantel)*
manufacture
  manufactured
  manufacturer
  manufacturing
many
map
  mapped
  mapping
maple
marble
  marbled
march *(to walk)*
  marches
March *(the month)*
margin
  marginal
mark
market
  marketable
marriage
  marriageable
marry
  married

Mars
marshal *(law officer)*
  [martial *(warlike)*]
martial *(see marshal)*
mask
Maryland
mass
  massed *(grouped)*
  [mast *(tall, straight pole)*]
masses
Massachusetts
mast *(tall, straight pole)*
  [massed *(grouped)*]
master
mat
match
  matches
mate
mated
  mating
material
  materialism
  materialize
mathematical
matter
maul *(mangle)*
  [mall *(courtyard)*]
may *(request or grant permission)*
May *(the month)*
maybe
mayor
maze *(confusing network of paths)*
  [maize *(Indian corn)*]

me

me
meadow
meal
mean *(irreg. vb.)*
meander
meaning
meantime
meanwhile
measure
  measured
  measuring
  measurement
meat *(animal flesh)*
  [meet *(greet)*]
  [mete *(to deal out)*]
mechanic
  mechanical

medal *(an award)*
  [meddle *(interfere)*]
meddle *(see medal)*
medicine
  medical
medieval
Mediterranean
medium
meek
meet *(greet)*
  [meat *(animal flesh)*]
  [mete *(to deal out)*]
melody
  melodic
melt
member
memento
memoir
memory
  memorable
  memories
Memphis
men
mental
  mentality
mention
  mentionable
merchant
mercury
mercy
mere
merry
  merrier
  merriest
  merrily
  merriment
mess
  messy
message
  messenger
met

metal *(iron, gold, etc.)*
  [mettle *(courage)*]
  metallic
mete *(to deal out)*
  [meat *(animal flesh)*]
  [meet *(greet)*]
meter
  metric
method
  methodical
  methodology
mettle *(courage)*
  [metal *(iron, gold, etc.)*]
Mexico
  Mexican

mi

mice
Michigan
microscope
  microscopic
middle
midnight
might *(1. may, 2. strength)*
  [mite *(small insect)*]
  mightier
  mightiest
  mightily
  mighty
mild
mile
mileage
military
milk
  milked
  milker
  milking
million
mill
Milwaukee
mind
mine
  mined
  miner *(coal digger)*
  [minor *(a juvenile)*]
  mining
mineral
mingle
  mingled
  mingling
miniature

minimum
  minimal
  minimize
ministry
  ministerial
  ministries
Minnesota
minor *(a juvenile)*
  [miner *(coal digger)*]
  minority
minus
minute
mirror
mischief
  mischievous
misconduct
misdemeanor
misery
  miserable
misfortune
miss
  missed *(did not contact)*
  [mist *(fog)*]
  misses
  missing
Mississippi
Missouri
misspell
mist *(fog)*
  [missed *(did not contact)*]
mistake
  mistakable
  mistaken
  mistaking
  mistook
mister *(Mr.)*
mite *(small insect)*
  [might *(1. may, 2. strength)*]
mix
  mixes
mixture

mo

moan *(groan)*
  [mown *(cut down)*]
mob
mobile
  mobility
mode *(the fashion)*
  [mowed *(cut down)*]
model

modem
modern
modify
  modifier
moist
  moisten
  moisture
mold
molecule
mom
moment
  momentarily
  momentary
  momentous
  momentum
Monday
money
  monetary
monkey
monotony
  monotonous
monster
  monstrosity
  monstrous
Montana
month
mood
  moodier
  moodiest
  moody
moon
  moonlike
  moonlight
  moonscape

The following regular endings are not in the word list and can be added to the root word without changes:
-ed, -er, -est, -ful, -ing, -less, -ly, -ness, and -s. Most exceptions and root changes are in the list.

moral *(concerned with right conduct)*
  [morale *(state of mind regarding cheerfulness)*]
  moralist
  morality
more
moreover
morn *(morning)*
  [mourn *(to grieve)*]
  morning
mosquito
  mosquitoes
moss
  mosses
most
moth
mother
motion
motor
  motorist
mount
mountain
  mountaineer
  mountainous
mountaintop
mourn *(to grieve)*
  [morn *(morning)*]
mouse
mouth
move
  movable
  moved
  movement
  moving
movie
moviegoer
moviemaker
mow *(irreg. vb.)*
  mowed *(cut down)*
  [mode *(the fashion)*]
  mown *(cut down)*
  [moan *(groan)*]

mu

much
mud
mug
  mugger
  mugging
mule
mull
multiple

multiply
  multiplication
multitude
mumble
mummy
murder
  murderer
  murderous
murmur
muscle *(part of the body)*
  [mussel *(shellfish)*]
museum
music
  musical
  musician
must
mustache
musty
  mustier
  mustiest
  mustiness
mutual

my

my
myself
mystery
  mysteries
  mysterious
  mysteriously
mystic
  mystical
myth
  mythical
  mythology

na

nail
name
  named
  naming
narrow
nation
  national
  nationalism
  nationalistic
  nationality
native
nature
  natural
naughty *(bad)*
  [knotty *(full of tangles)*]

navy
  naval *(nautical)*
  [navel *(depression in stomach)*]
  navies
nay *(no)*
  [neigh *(horse's whinnying sound)*]

ne

near
nearby
neat
Nebraska
necessary
  necessarily
necessity
neck
need *(require)*
  [knead *(mix with hands)*]
needle
  needled
  needling
negative
  negativity
neigh *(horse's whinnying sound)*
  [nay *(no)*]
Negro
neighbor
neighborhood
neither
nerve
  nervous
nest
net
  netted
  netting
Netherland
  Netherlander
Nevada
never
nevertheless

new *(opposite of old)*
   [**gnu** *(African antelope)*]
   [**knew** *(did know)*]
New Hampshire
New Jersey
New Mexico
New Orleans
New York
New Zealand
newspaper
next

ni

nice
   nicer
   nicest
niche
nickel
niece
night *(evening)*
   [**knight** *(servant of a king)*]
nine
   ninth
nineteen
   nineteenth
ninety
   nineties
   ninetieth
nit *(louse egg)*
   [**knit** *(weave with yarn)*]

no

no *(expression of refusal)*
   [**know** *(familiar with)*]
noble
   nobility
   nobly
nobody
   nobodies
nod
   nodded
   nodding
noise
   noisier
   noisiest
   noisily
   noisy
none *(not any)*
   [**nun** *(Catholic sister)*]
nonsense
noon

noonday
noontime
nor
normal
   normality
   normally
north *(direction)*
North *(geographical area)*
North Carolina
North Dakota
northeast
   northeastern
northwest
   northwestern
Norway
   Norwegian
nose
   nosed
   nosing
nostalgia
   nostalgic
   nostalgically
not *(in no manner)*
   [**knot** *(tangle)*]
note
   notable
   notation
notebook
nothing
notice
   noticeable
notion
notorious
noun
nourish
   nourishment
November
now
nowhere

nu

nuclear
number
numeral
   numerical
numerator
numerous
nun *(Catholic sister)*
   [**none** *(not any)*]
nurse
   nursed
   nursing

nut
nutrient
   nutrition
   nutritious

oa

oak
oar *(paddle for a boat)*
   [**or** *(word used to show choices)*]
   ore *(mineral deposit)*
oat

ob

obey
   obedience
   obedient
object
   objectify
   objection
   objective
obligate
   obligation
   obligatory
oblige
oblong
observe
   observable
   observant
   observation
   observatory
obtain
obvious

The following regular endings are not in the word list and can be added to the root word without changes:
-ed, -er, -est, -ful, -ing, -less, -ly, -ness, and -s. Most exceptions and root changes are in the list.

oc

occasion
  occasionally
occupy
  occupied
  occupies
occur
  occurred
  occurrence
  occurring
ocean
o'clock *(of the clock)*
October

od

odd
ode *(a poem)*
  [owed *(did owe)*]
odor

of

of *(derived or coming from)*
off *(opposite of on)*
offal *(entrails)*
  [awful *(terrible)*]
offer
office
  officer
  official
offshore
often

oh

oh *(an exclamation)*
  [owe *(be indebted)*]
Ohio
oil
oilcan
oilcloth

ok

Oklahoma

ol

old
olive
Olympic
  Olympiad

om

omit
  omitted
  omitting

on

on
once
one *(the number 1)*
  [won *(triumphed)*]
ongoing
onion
only
onto
onshore
onstage
onward

op

open
opera
operate
  operation
  operational
  operator
opinion
  opinionated
opportune
  opportunist
  opportunity
  opportunities
oppose
opposite
  opposition
oppress
  oppression
  oppressive
option
  optional
  optionally

or

or *(word used to show choices)*
  [oar *(paddle for a boat)*]
  [ore *(mineral deposit)*]
ore *(see or)*
Oregon
organ
organism

organize
  organization
origin
  original
  originality
  originate

ot

other
otherwise

ou

ought
ounce
our *(belonging to us)*
  [hour *(60-minute period)*]
ourselves
out
outdoors
outer
outline
  outlined
  outlining
outside

ov

oven
over
overall
overboard
overcoat
overcome
  overcame
  overcoming
overdo *(go to extremes)*
  [overdue *(a bill not paid on time)*]
overhead
overhear
overlap
overlay
overlook
overnight

overpower
overseas *(abroad)*
   [oversees *(supervises)*]

OW

owe *(be indebted)*
   [oh *(an exclamation)*]
   owed *(did owe)*
   [ode *(a poem)*]
owl
own

OX

ox
   oxen
oxygen
   oxygenate

oy

oyster

oz

ozone

pa

pa
pace
Pacific
pack
   packed *(did pack)*
   [pact *(agreement)*]
package
pact *(agreement)*
   [packed *(did pack)*]
pad
paddle
page
paid
pail *(bucket)*
   [pale *(light in color)*]
pain *(discomfort)*
   [pane *(window glass)*]
painstakingly
paint
pair *(two of a kind)*
   [pare *(to peel)*]
   [pear *(a fruit)*]
Pakistan
   Pakistani
palace

palate *(roof of mouth)*
   [palette *(board that holds artist's paint)*]
   [pallet *(shovel-like tool)*]
pale *(light in color)*
   [pail *(bucket)*]
palette *(board that holds artist's paint)*
   [palate *(roof of mouth)*]
   [pallet *(shovel-like tool)*]
palm
pan
Panama
pane *(window glass)*
   [pain *(discomfort)*]
pants
papa
paper
parade
   paraded
   parading
paragraph
Paraguay
   Paraguayan
parallel
parallelogram
pare *(to peal)*
   [pair *(two of a kind)*]
   [pear *(a fruit)*]
parent
parenthesis
   parentheses
   parenthetic
Paris
park
parody
   parodied
parrot
part
   partial
participate
   participation
   participator
   participatory
participle
particle
particular
partition
partner
party
   parties

pass
   passed *(moved by)*
   [past *(former time)*]
passage
passageway
passenger
passerby
   passersby
past *(former time)*
   [passed *(moved by)*]
paste
pasture
pat
patch
   patches
path
patience *(ability to endure)*
   [patients *(sick persons)*]
patient
   patients *(sick persons)*
   [patience *(ability to endure)*]
pattern
pause *(brief stop)*
   [paws *(feet of animals)*]
paws *(see pause)*
pay *(irreg. vb.)*

pe

peace *(tranquility)*
   [piece *(part of a whole)*]

The following regular endings are not in the word list and can be added to the root word without changes:
-ed, -er, -est, -ful, -ing, -less, -ly, -ness, and -s. Most exceptions and root changes are in the list.

peach
  peaches
peak *(mountaintop)*
  [peek *(sneak a look)*]
  [pique *(spark interest)*]
peal *(ringing sound)*
  [peel *(skin or rind of fruit)*]
peanut
pear *(a fruit)*
  [pair *(two of a kind)*]
  [pare *(to peel)*]
pearl *(jewel)*
  [purl *(knitting stitch)*]
peculiar
pedal *(ride a bike)*
  [peddle *(sell)*]
peddle *(see pedal)*
peek *(sneak a look)*
  [peak *(mountaintop)*]
  [pique *(spark interest)*]
peel *(skin or rind of fruit)*
  [peal *(ringing sound)*]
peer *(an equal)*
  [pier *(a dock)*]
pen
pencil
peninsula
Pennsylvania
penny
  pennies
  penniless
people
  peopled
pepper
per *(for each)*
  [purr *(cat sound)*]
percent
  percentage
perfect
perform
  performance
perhaps
perimeter
period
  periodical
permanent
  permanence
permit
  permitted
  permitting
perpendicular
persecute

persevere
  perseverance
  persevered
  preserving
person
personal *(of one person)*
  [personnel *(employees)*]
personality
  personalities
personnel *(employees)*
  [personal *(of one person)*]
persuade
  persuaded
  persuading
Peru
  Peruvian
pet
  petted
  petting

ph

phase *(a stage)*
  [faze *(upset)*]
Philadelphia
  Philadelphian
Philippines
  Filipino
Phoenix
photograph
  photographic
  photography
phrase
  phrased
  phrasing
physical
physician

pi

pi *(a Greek letter)*
  [pie *(type of pastry)*]
piano
  pianist
pick
picnic
  picnicked
  picnicker
  picnicking
picture
  pictured
  picturing
pie *(type of pastry)*
  [pi *(a Greek letter)*]

piece *(part of a whole)*
  [peace *(tranquility)*]
pieced
  piecing
pier *(a dock)*
  [peer *(an equal)*]
pig
pigeon
pile
  piled
  piling
pilgrim
  pilgrimage
pilot
pin
  pinned
  pinning
pinch
  pinches
pink
pioneer
pipe
  piped
  piping
pique *(spark interest)*
  [peak *(mountaintop)*]
  [peek *(sneak a look)*]
pirate
  piracy
  pirated
  pirating
pit
pitch
  pitches
pity
  pitiable
  pitiably
  pitied
  pities
  pitiful
  pitiless

place
  placed
  placing
plain *(not fancy)*
  [plane *(flat surface)*]
plaintive
plait *(braid)*
  [plate *(dish)*]
plan
  planned
  planner
  planning
plane *(flat surface)*
  [plain *(not fancy)*]
  planed
  planing
planet
  planetarium
  planetary
plant
plastic
  plasticity
plate *(dish)*
  [plait *(braid)*]
  plated
  plating
plateau
  plateaus or plateaux
platform
platitude
Plato
  platonic
platoon
play
playground
playmate
playwright
plaza
pleasant
please *(to make glad)*
  [pleas *(appeals)*]
pleasure
  pleasurable
plenty
  plentiful
plot
  plotted
  plotting
plow
plug
plum *(a fruit)*
  [plumb *(a lead weight)*]

plumb *(see plum)*
plunder
plural
plus

po

pocket
poem
poet
  poetic
poetry
poignant
point
  pointy
poise
  poised
poison
  poisonous
Poland
  Polish
polar
pole *(a stick)*
  [poll *(an election)*]
  poled
  poling
police
  policed
  policing
policeman
  policemen
policewoman
  policewomen
policy
  policies
polish
polite
politics
  political
poll *(an election)*
  [pole *(a stick)*]
pollen
polyester
polygraph
pond
ponder
  ponderous
pony
  ponies
pool
poor

pop
  popped
  popping
popular
  popularity
population
porch
pore *(tiny opening in skin)*
  [pour *(to make liquid flow)*]
port
portion
portrait
portray
Portugal
  Portugese
pose
  posed
  poser
  posing
position
positive
possess
  possession
  possessive
possible
  possibilities
  possibility
  possibly
post
pot
  potted
  potter
  potting
potato
  potatoes
potent
potential
pottery
pound
pour *(to make liquid flow)*
  [pore *(tiny opening in skin)*]
powder
power

The following regular endings are not in the word list and can be added to the root word without changes:
-ed, -er, -est, -ful, -ing, -less, -ly, -ness, and -s. Most exceptions and root changes are in the list.

pr

practical
practice
 practiced
 practicing
prairie
praise
 praised
 praising
praiseworthy
 praiseworthiness
pray *(worship)*
 [prey *(animal hunted for food)*]
prayer
precede *(come before)*
 [proceed *(go forward)*]
 preceded
 preceding
precious
precise
predicate
 predicated
prefer
 preference
 preferential
 preferred
 preferring
prefix
 prefixes
prepare
 preparation
 prepared
 preparing
preposition
 prepositional
presence
present *(1. to give, 2. stage a play or show)*
present *(1. a gift, 2. the time now, 3. in attendance)*
president
 presidential
press
pressure
 pressured
 pressuring
presume
 presumed
 presuming
 presumption

pretend
 pretense
 pretension
 pretentious
pretty
 prettied
 prettier
 pretties
 prettiest
 prettily
 prettiness
prevail
 prevalence
 prevalent
prevent
 prevention
previous
prey *(animal hunted for food)*
 [pray *(worship)*]
price
 priced
 pricey
 pricing
prickly
 pricklier
 prickliest
 prickliness
pride *(self-esteem)*
 [pried *(1. inquired in a nosey way, 2. moved with a lever)*]
 prided
 priding
priest
priestess
prim
primal
primary
 primaries
 primarily
primate
prime
 primed
 priming
primitive
prince
princess
 princesses
principal *(1. most important, 2. head of school)*
 [principle *(fundamental law)*]
principle *(see principal)*
print

prior
priority
 priorities
prison
pristine
private
privilege
 privileged
prize
 prized
probable
 probabilities
 probability
 probably
problem
 problematic
proceed *(go forward)*
 [precede *(come before)*]
 procedure
process
prodigious
produce
 produced
 producer
 producing
product
 production
 productive
 productivity
profession
 professional
professor
profit *(gain in money)*
 [prophet *(seer; visionary)*]
profound
program
 programmed
 programmer
 programming
progress
prohibit
 prohibitive
project
promise
 promised
 promising
promote
 promoted
 promoter
 promoting
 promotion
 promotional
pronoun

pronounce
  pronounced
  pronouncing
  pronunciation
proofread
propaganda
  propagandist
  propagandize
  propagandized
  propagandizing
propel
  propelled
  propelling
  propeller
proper
property
  properties
prophet *(seer; visionary)*
  [profit *(gain in money)*]
proportion
propose
  proposal
proposition
prose
prosecute
  prosecuted
  prosecuting
  prosecution
  prosecutor
prosper
  prosperous
protect
  protection
  protective
protein
proud
prove
  proved
  proven
  proving
provide
  provided
  providing
province
pry
  pried *(1. inquired in a nosey way, 2. moved with a lever)*
  [pride *(self-esteem)*]

ps
pseudonym
psychiatry
  psychiatric
  psychiatrist
psychology
  psychologist

pu
public
publicity
  publicist
publish
  publication
pull
pump
punctuate
punish
  punishment
pupil
puppy
  puppies
purchase
  purchased
  purchaser
  purchasing
pure
  purer
  purest
  purity
purl *(knitting stitch)*
  [pearl *(jewel)*]
purple
  purplish
purpose
purr *(cat sound)*
  [per *(for each)*]
pursue
  pursued
  pursuing
push
  pushes
put *(irreg. vb.)*
  putting
puzzle
  puzzled
  puzzling

py
pyramid
pyre
python

qu
qualify
  qualified
  qualifier
  qualifies
quality
  qualities
quantify
  quantified
  quantifies
quantity
  quantities
quantify
quart
  quarts *(measure)*
  [quartz *(mineral)*]
quarter
quarterback
quartet
quartz *(mineral)*
  [quarts *(measure)*]
queasy
  queasier
  queasiest
  queasiness
queen
queer
quench
  quenches
question
queue *(line of people)*
  [cue *(to prompt)*]
quick
  quicken
quiet *(silent)*
quite *(positively)*
quiver
quiz
  quizzed
  quizzes
  quizzical
  quizzically
  quizzing

The following regular endings are not in the word list and can be added to the root word without changes: -ed, -er, -est, -ful, -ing, -less, -ly, -ness, and -s. Most exceptions and root changes are in the list.

quota
quote
  quotable
  quotation
  quoted
  quoting
quotient

ra
rabbi
rabbit
raccoon
race
  raced
  racer
  racing
radiation
radical
  radicalism
radio
radioactive
  radioactivity
radius
raft
rag
rage
  raged
  raging
rail
railroad
rain *(precipitation)*
  [reign *(royal rule)*]
  [rein *(harness)*]
  rainier
  rainiest
  rainy
rainfall
raise *(put up)*
  [raze *(tear down)*]
  [rays *(beams of energy)*]
  raised
  raising
rampant
ran *(irreg. vb.)*
ranch
  rancher
  ranches
  ranching
rang
range
  ranged
  ranger
  ranging

rank
  ranked
  ranking
rap *(hit)*
  [wrap *(cover)*]
  rapped
  rapping
rapid
  rapidity
rare
  rarely
  rarer
  rarest
  rarity
rat
rate
  rated
  rater
  rating
rather
ratio
ration
  rational
  rationalism
  rationalize
  rationally
rationale
rat
raw
ray
  rays *(beams of energy)*
  [raise *(put up)*]
  [raze *(tear down)*]
raze *(see ray)*

re
reach
  reaches
react
  reaction
  reactionary
  reactor
read *(scan printed matter)*
  (irreg. vb.)
  [reed *(a plant)*]
  reader
  reading
read *(have scanned printed
  material)*
  [red *(a color)*]
ready
  readied
  readying

real *(genuine)*
  [reel *(spool)*]
  realism
  realities
  reality
realize
  realization
  realized
  realizing
rear
  reared
  rearing
reason
  reasonable
  reasonably
rebel
  rebelled
  rebelling
  rebellion
  rebellious
recall
receipt
receive
  received
  receiver
  receiving
recent
receptacle
reception
  receptionist
  receptive
recipe
recipient
reciprocate
  reciprocal
  reciprocated
  reciprocating
recognize
  recognition
  recognizable
  recognizance
  recognized
  recognizing
recollect
  recollection
recommend
  recommendation
recompense
  recompensed
  recompensing

reconcile
  reconciled
  reconciliation
  reconciling
record
recover
rectangle
  rectangular
rectify
  rectified
  rectifies
  rectifying
red *(a color)*
  [read *(have scanned printed matter)*]
  redder
  reddest
  redness
reduce
  reduced
  reducing
  reduction
reed *(a plant)*
  [read *(scan printed matter)*]
reek *(give off strong odor)*
  [wreak *(inflict)*]
reel *(spool)*
  [real *(genuine)*]
refer
  reference
  referral
  referred
  referring
referendum
  referenda
reflect
  reflection
  reflector
refrigerate
  refrigeration
  refrigerator
refuse
  refused
  refusing
regard
region
  regional
  regionalism
regret
  regrettable
  regretted
  regretting

regular
reign *(royal rule)*
  [rain *(precipitation)*]
  [rein *(harness)*]
relate
  related
  relating
relation
  relationship
relative
  relativism
  relativity
relax
  relaxation
release
  released
  releasing
relief
  relieve
  relieved
  relieving
religion
  religiosity
  religious
remain
remarkable
  remarkably
remember
  remembrance
remind
reminisce
  reminiscence
  reminiscent
  reminiscing
remiss
  remission
remit
  remitted
  remitter
  remitting
remorse
remote
  remoter
  remotest
remove
  removable
  removed
  remover
  removing
rename
rendezvous

renounce
  renounced
  renouncing
  renunciation
rent
recognize
  recognizable
  recognition
  recognized
  recognizer
  recognizing
repair
repeal
repeat
  repetition
  repetitious
repel
  repelled
  repellent
  repelling
repent
  repentance
  repentant
repercussion
repertoire
  repertory
repetition
  repetitious
replace
  replaceable
  replaced
  replacement
  replacing
replicate
  replicated
  replicating
  replication
reply
  replied
report
represent
  representation
  representative
reprieve
  reprieved
  reprieving
reproach

The following regular endings are not in the word list and can be added to the root word without changes:
-ed, -er, -est, -ful, -ing, -less, -ly, -ness, and -s. Most exceptions and root changes are in the list.

reptile
  reptilian
republic
  republican
repudiate
  repudiated
  repudiating
  repudiation
repulse
  repulsed
  repulsing
  repulsion
reputation
repute
require
  required
  requirement
  requiring
requisite
  requisition
rescue
  rescued
  rescuer
  rescuing
research
resemble
  resemblance
  resembled
  resembling
resist
  resistance
  resistant
resolute
  resolution
resolve
  resolved
  resolving
resonant
  resonance
resource
respect
  respectability
  respectably
  respectfully
  respective
respond
  responsive
responsible
  responsibility
  responsibilities
rest *(relax)*
  [wrest *(take from)*]
restaurant
  restaurateur

restless
result
  resultant
resume *(take up again)*
  resumed
  resuming
  resumption
resume *(short account of one's career)*
resurrect
  resurrection
retain
retaliate
  retaliated
retention
  retentive
reticent
  reticence
retinue
retire
retort
return
  returnable
reveal
  revelation
reverend
review
revolt
revolution
  revolutionary
reward
rewrite
  rewriting
  rewritten
  rewrote

rh

Rhine River
rhinoceros
Rhode Island
rhyme *(repetition of same sounds)*
  [rime *(type of ice; frost)*]
  rhymed
  rhymer
  rhyming
rhythm
  rhythmic
  rhythmical

ri

rib
  ribbed
  ribbing
ribbon
rice
rich
  riches
ride *(irreg. vb.)*
  rider
  riding
ridge
ridicule
  ridiculous
rifle
  rifled
  rifling
right *(correct)*
  [rite *(ceremony)*]
  [write *(inscribe)*]
rigid
rime *(type of ice; frost)*
  [rhyme *(repitition of same sounds)*]
ring *(circular band)*
  [wring *(squeeze)*]
ring *(irreg. vb.)*
rink
riot
rip
  ripped
  ripping
ripe
  ripen
rise *(irreg. vb.)*
  risen
  rising
risk
  risky
rite *(ceremony)*
  [right *(correct)*]
  [write *(inscribe)*]

rival
  rivalry
  rivalries
river

ro

road *(street)*
  [rode *(traveled)*]
  [rowed *(used oars)*]
roar
robot
  robotic
rock
  rocky
rocket
rode *(traveled)*
  [road *(street)*]
  [rowed *(used oars)*]
roe *(fish eggs)*
  [row *(1. a line, 2. use oars)*]
role *(a part played)*
  [roll *(1. turn over, 2. bread)*]
Rome
  Roman
romance
  romanced
  romancing
  romantic
  romantically
root *(part of a plant)*
  [route *(roadway)*]
rope
  roped
  roper
  roping
rose *(type of flower)*
  [rows *(1. lines, 2. uses oars)*]
rote *(by memory)*
  [wrote *(did write)*]
rough *(not smooth)*
  [ruff *(pleated collar)*]
round
route *(roadway)*
  [root *(part of a plant)*]
  routed
  routing
row *(1. a line, 2 use oars)*
  [roe *(fish eggs)*]
  rowed *(used oars)*
  [road *(street)*]
  [rode *(traveled)*]
royal

ru

rub
  rubbed
  rubbing
rubber
  rubbery
ruby
rude *(impolite)*
  [rued *(regretted)*]
ruse *(subterfuge)*
rug
  rugged
rule
  ruled
  ruler
  ruling
Rumania
  Rumanian
rumor
run *(irreg. vb.)*
  runner
  running
runaway
rung *(a step on a ladder)*
  [wrung *(squeezed)*]
ruse *(subterfuge)*
  [rues *(regret)*]
rush
  rushes
Russia
  Russian
rust
  rusty

ry

rye *(grain)*
  [wry *(ironically humorous)*]

sa

sack
sacrifice
sad
  sadden
  sadder
  saddest
saddle
  saddled
  saddling
safe

safer
safest
safety
safeties
said
sail *(travel by boat)*
  [sale *(selling at bargain prices)*]
sailor
saint
salad
sale *(selling at bargain prices)*
  [sail *(travel by boat)*]
salmon
salt
  saltier
  saltiest
  salty
salute
  salutation
  saluted
  saluting
same
sample
  sampled
  sampler
  sampling
San Antonio
San Diego
San Francisco
San Jose
sand
  sandy

The following regular endings are not in the word list and can be added to the root word without changes: -ed, -er, -est, -ful, -ing, -less, -ly, -ness, and -s. Most exceptions and root changes are in the list.

sandal
sandwich
  sandwiches
sang
sank
Santa Claus
sap
sash
sat
satellite
satin
satisfy
  satisfaction
  satisfactory
  satisfied
Saturday
sauce
  saucer
  saucy
save
  saved
  saver
  saving
saw
say *(irreg. vb.)*

sc
scale
  scaled
  scaling
scar
scarce
  scarcer
  scarcest
  scarcity
scare
  scared
  scarier
  scariest
  scaring
  scary
scarf
  scarves
scatter
scene *(setting)*
  [seen *(viewed)*]
scent *(odor)*
  [cent *(penny)*]
  [sent *(did send)*]
schedule
  scheduled
  scheduling
scholar
  scholarship

school
science
  scientific
  scientifically
  scientist
scissors
scold
scoop
scoot
  scooter
scope
scorch
  scorches
score
  scored
  scorer
  scoring
scout
scraggly
scramble
  scrambled
  scrambling
scrap
  scrapped
  scrapping
scratch
  scratches
  scratchy
scrawl
scrawny
  scrawnier
  scrawniest
scream
screech
  screeches
screen
screenplay
screenwriter
screw
screwdriver
scribble
  scribbled
  scribbler
  scribbling
scrimp
script
scroll
scrub
  scrubbed
  scrubbier
  scrubbiest
  scrubbing
  scrubby
scruff

scuff
  scuffed
  scuffing
scull *(racing boat)*
  [skull *(the head)*]
sculpt
  sculptor
  sculpture
  sculpturing
scum
  scummed
  scumming
  scummy
scurry

se
sea *(ocean)*
  [see *(visualize)*]
seal
sealing *(closing)*
  [ceiling *(top of room)*]
seam *(where two pieces join)*
  [seem *(give the impression of being)*]
  seamy
sear *(singe)*
  [seer *(prophet; visionary)*]
search
  searches
season
  seasonable
  seasonal
seat
Seattle
seaward
second
  secondary
secret
  secrecy
  secretive
secretary
  secretarial
  secretaries
section
  sectional

secure
  secured
  securing
security
  securities
sedate
  sedated
  sedating
  sedative
see *(visualize) (irreg. vb.)*
  [sea *(ocean)*]
seed *(part of a plant)*
  [cede *(give over; surrender)*]
seek *(irreg. vb.)*
seem *(give the impression of being)*
  [seam *(where two pieces join)*]
seen *(viewed)*
  [scene *(setting)*]
seer *(prophet; visionary)*
  [sear *(singe)*]
segment
seize
  seized
  seizes
  seizing
  seizure
seldom
select
  selection
  selective
self
  selves
sell *(exchange for money) (irreg. vb.)*
  [cell *(prison room)*]
  seller *(one who sells)*
  [cellar *(basement)*]
semester
senate
  senator
send *(irreg. vb.)*
  sent *(did send)*
  [cent *(penny)*]
  [scent *(odor)*]
senior
  seniority

sense *(feel)*
  [cents *(pennies)*]
  sensed
  sensing
  sensitive
sensible
  sensibility
  sensibly
sensor *(detection device)*
  [censor *(to ban)*]
  sensory
sent *(did send)*
  [cent *(penny)*]
  [scent *(smell)*]
sentence
  sentenced
  sentencing
separate
  separated
  separating
  separation
September
serf *(feudal servant)*
  [surf *(ocean waves)*]
sergeant
series
  serial *(of a series)*
  [cereal *(food made from grain)*]
serious
serpent
  serpentine
servant
serve
  served
  server
  serving
service
  serviced
  servicing
session *(a meeting)*
  [cession *(yielding)*]
set
  setting
settle
  settled
  settlement
  settler
  settles
  settling

seven
  seventh
seventeen
  seventeenth
seventy
  seventies
  seventieth
several
severe
  severity
sew *(mend) (irreg. vb.)*
  [so *(in order that)*]
  [sow *(plant seeds)*]
sewage
sewer
sewn

sh

shabby
  shabbier
  shabbiest
  shabbily
  shabbiness
shackle
  shackled
  shackling
shade
  shaded
  shadier
  shadiest
  shading
  shady
shadow
  shadowy
shaft
shake *(irreg. vb.)*
  shaken
  shaker
  shakier
  shakiest
  shaking
  shaky
shall
shallow
shamble *(walk awkwardly or unsteadily)*
  shambled
  shambling
shambles *(confusion; a mess)*

The following regular endings are not in the word list and can be added to the root word without changes: -ed, -er, -est, -ful, -ing, -less, -ly, -ness, and -s. Most exceptions and root changes are in the list.

shame
  shamed
  shaming
shamefaced
shampoo
shape
  shaped
  shapeliest
  shaping
share
  shared
  sharer
  sharing
shark
sharp
shave
  shaved
  shaven
  shaver
  shaving
shear *(cut)*
  [sheer *(transparent)*]
shed
  shedding
she
she'd *(she had, she would)*
sheep
sheer *(transparent)*
  [shear *(cut)*]
sheet
sheik *(Arab chief)*
  [chic *(stylish)*]
shelf
  shelved
  shelves
  shelving
shell
she'll *(she will)*
shelter
shepherd
sheriff
she's *(she has, she is)*
shield
shift
  shiftier
  shiftiest
  shiftiness
  shifty
shine *(irreg. vb.)*
  shinier
  shiniest
  shining
  shiny

ship
  shipped
  shipping
shirt
shock
shoe *(foot covering)*
  [shoo *(chase away)*]
shone *(beamed)*
  [shown *(exhibited)*]
shoo *(chase away)*
  [shoe *(foot covering)*]
shook *(irreg. vb.)*
shoot *(discharge gun)*
  [chute *(slide)*]
shop
  shopped
  shopper
  shopping
shore
  shored
  shoring
short
shot
shotgun
should
shoulder
shout
shovel
show *(irreg. vb.)*
  shown *(exhibited)*
  [shone *(beamed)*]
showcase
  showcased
  showcasing
shower
showroom
shrank
shred
shriek
shrill
shrink *(irreg. vb.)*
  shrinkage
shrug
  shrugged
  shrugging
shrunk
shuffle
  shuffled
  shuffling
shut *(irreg. vb.)*
  shutting
shy
  shier
  shiest

si
Siam
  Siamese
sick
  sicken
  sickening
side *(flank)*
  [sighed *(breathed audibly)*]
  sided
  siding
sidewalk
sideways
sigh
  sighed *(breathed audibly)*
  [side *(flank)*]
  sighs *(audible breaths)*
  [size *(physical dimension)*]
sight *(vision)*
  [cite *(give credit to a source)*]
  [site *(location)*]
sign *(signal)*
  [sine *(trigonometric function)*]
signal
signature
significant
  significance
silent
  silence
  silenced
  silencer
  silencing
silk
  silken
  silky
silly
  sillier
  silliest
  silliness

silver
  silvery
similar
  similarities
  similarity
simile
simmer
simper
simple
  simpler
  simplest
  simplicity
  simply
simplify
  simplified
  simplifies
simulate
  simulated
  simulating
  simulation
simultaneous
since
sine *(trigonometric function)*
  [sign *(signal)*]
sing *(irreg. vb.)*
single
  singled
  singling
singular
  singularity
  singularities
sink *(irreg. vb.)*
sip
  sipped
  sipping
sir
sister
sit *(irreg. vb.)*
  sitter
  sitting
site *(location)*
  [cite *(give credit to a source)*]
  [sight *(vision)*]
situate
  situated
  situating
  situation
  situational
six
  sixes
  sixth

sixteen
  sixteenth
sixty
  sixties
  sixtieth
size *(physical dimensional)*
  [sighs *(audible breaths)*]
  sized
  sizing

sk

skate
skeleton
  skeletal
skeptic
  skeptical
  skepticism
sketch
ski
  skiing
skid
  skidded
  skidding
skill
skin
  skinned
  skinning
skip
  skipped
  skipper
  skipping
skirt
skull *(the head)*
  [scull *(racing boat)*]
skunk
sky
  skies

sl

slack
  slacken
slam
  slammed
  slamming
slang
slant
slap
  slapped
  slapping

slave
  slaved
  slavery
  slaving
slay *(kill)*
  [sleigh *(sled)*]
sled
  sledded
  sledding
sleep *(irreg. vb.)*
  sleepier
  sleepiest
  sleepily
  sleepiness
  sleepy
  slept
sleeve
sleigh *(sled)*
  [slay *(kill)*]
sleight *(skill)*
  [slight *(slender)*]
slice
  sliced
  slicing
slid
slide *(irreg. vb.)*
  slider
  sliding
slight *(slender)*
  [sleight *(skill)*]
slim
  slimmer
  slimmest
  slimming
slip
  slipped
  slippery
  slipping
slope
  sloped
  sloping
sloppy
  sloppier
  sloppiest

The following regular endings are not in the word list and can be added to the root word without changes: -ed, -er, -est, -ful, -ing, -less, -ly, -ness, and -s. Most exceptions and root changes are in the list.

slot
  slotted
  slotting
slow
slug
  slugged
  slugging
  sluggish
slumber
slump

sm

small
smart
  smarten
smash
smear
smell
  smellier
  smelliest
  smelly
smile
  smiled
  smiling
smoke
  smoked
  smoker
  smoking
  smoky
smooth
smother

sn

snack
snag
  snagged
  snagging
snake
  snaked
  snaking
snap
  snapped
  snapping
  snappy
sneak
sneeze
sniff
snip
  snipped
  snipping
  snippy
snore
  snored
  snoring

snow
  snowy
snowball
snowfall
snowflake
snowman
snowstorm
snub
  snubbed
  snubbing
snuggle

so

so *(in order that)*
  [sew *(mend)*]
  [sow *(plant seeds)*]
soak
soap
  soapy
soar *(fly)*
  [sore *(painful)*]
social
society
  societies
sock
soda
sofa
soft
soil
sold *(did sell)*
  [soled *(bottom placed on a shoe)*]
sole *(1. only, 2. bottom of foot)*
  soul *(spirit)*
solicit
  solicitor
solid
solution
solve
  solved
  solving
some *(a portion)*
  [sum *(total)*]
somebody
someday
somehow
someone
something
sometime *(unspecified)*
sometimes *(on some occasions)*
somewhat
somewhere

son *(male offspring)*
  [sun *(a star)*]
song
soon
sore *(painful)*
  [soar *(fly)*]
sought
sorry
  sorrier
  sorriest
sort
soul *(spirit)*
  sole *(1. only, 2. bottom of foot)*
sound
soup
sour
source
south *(direction)*
South *(geographical area)*
South Africa
South Carolina
South Dakota
southeast
  southeastern
southern
  southernmost
southwest
  southwestern
Soviet
sow *(plant seeds) (irreg. vb.)*
  [sew *(mend)*]
  [so *(in order that)*]
  sown

sp

space
  spaced
  spacing
  spacious
Spain
  Spaniard
  Spanish

spare
  spared
  sparing
spark
spasm
speak *(irreg. vb.)*
spear
special
species
specific
  specifically
specify
  specified
  specifies
speech
  speeches
speed
  sped
  speedier
  speediest
  speediness
  speedy
spell
spend *(irreg. vb.)*
spent
sphere
spider
spill
  spilt
spin *(irreg. vb.)*
  spinner
  spinning
spiral
spirit
spit *(irreg. vb.)*
spite
splash
  splashes
split *(irreg. vb.)*
  splitting
spoil
  spoilt
spoke *(1. did speak, 2. part of a wheel)*
  spoken
spoon
sport
spot
  spotted
  spotting
sprang

spread *(irreg. vb.)*
spring *(irreg. vb.)*
sprinkle
spun
sprung

sq
square
  squared
  squaring
squeak
squeeze
  squeezed
  squeezing
squirm
squirrel
squirt

st
stab
  stabbed
  stabbing
stability
  stabilities
stabilize
  stabilized
  stabilizer
  stabilizing
stable
  stabler
  stablest
stack
stadium
staff
stage
  staged
  staging
staid *(proper)*
  [stayed *(remained)*]
stain
stair *(a step)*
  [stare *(look intently)*]
stake *(post)*
  [steak *(cut of beef)*]
stall
stamp
stand *(irreg. vb.)*
standard
stanza

star
  starred
  starring
  starry
starboard
stardom
stardust
stare *(look intently)*
  [stair *(a step)*]
  stared
  staring
starfish
starry
  starrier
  starriest
start
state
  stated
  stating
  statement
station
stationary *(in a fixed position)*
  [stationery *(writing paper)*]
statistic
  statistical
  statistically
  statistician
statue
stay
  stayed *(remained)*
  [staid *(proper)*]
steady
  steadied
  steadier
  steadies
  steadiest
  steadily
  steadiness
steak *(cut of beef)*
  [stake *(post)*]
steal *(rob) (irreg. vb.)*
  [steel *(metal)*]
steam
  steamy
steel *(metal)*
  [steal *(rob)*]

The following regular endings are not in the word list and can be added to the root word without changes: -ed, -er, -est, -ful, -ing, -less, -ly, -ness, and -s. Most exceptions and root changes are in the list.

steep
steeple
steer
stem
  stemmed
  stemming
step *(walk)*
  [steppe *(prairie)*]
  stepped
  stepping
stereo
stereotype
  stereotypical
stern
stick *(irreg. vb.)*
  sticky
stiff
stile *(gate)*
  [style *(fashion)*]
still
sting
stir
  stirred
  stirring
stitch
  stitches
stock
  stocked
  stocking
stole
  stolen
stomach
stone
  stoned
  stoning
stood
stop
  stopped
  stopper
  stopping
store
  stored
  storing
stormy
story
  stories
stove
straight *(not crooked)*
  [strait *(channel of water)*]
strain
strait *(channel of water)*
  [straight *(not crooked)*]

strange
  stranger
  strangest
strategy
  strategies
straw
streak
stream
streamline
  streamlined
  streamliner
street
strength
  strengthen
stress
  stresses
stretch
  stretches
stride *(irreg. vb.)*
  striding
strike *(irreg. vb.)*
  striker
  striking
string *(irreg. vb.)*
strip
  stripped
  stripper
  stripping
strode
stroke
  stroked
  stroking
strong
struck
structure
  structured
  structuring
struggle
  struggled
  struggling
strung
stubborn
stuck
student
study
  studied
stuff
stung
stupid
style *(fashion)*
  [stile *(gate)*]
  styled
  styling

su
subject
submarine
  submariner
submerge
  submerged
  submerging
submerse
  submersed
  submersing
subset
subtle
  subtler
  subtlest
  subtleties
  subtlety
  subtly
substance
substitute
  substituted
  substituting
  substitution
subtract
  subtraction
succeed
success
  successes
  succession
  successive
  successor
succinct
succumb
such
sudden
sue
suffer
suffice
  sufficed
  sufficient
  sufficing
suffix
  suffixes
sugar
  sugary
suggest
  suggestion
  suggestive

suit
suitable
   suitability
   suitably
suite *(connected rooms)*
   [sweet *(sugary)*]
sum *(total)*
   [some *(a portion)*]
   summed
   summing
summer
sun (a *star*)
   [son *(male offspring)*]
   sunned
   sunnier
   sunniest
   sunning
   sunny
Sunday
sung
sunk
sunlight
sunrise
sunset
sunshine
suntan
   suntanned
   suntanning
super
superficial
superior
supermarket
supersede
   superseded
   superseding
supervise
   supervision
   supervisor
   supervisory
supine
supper
supply
   supplied
   supplier
   supplies
support
suppose
   supposed
   supposing
supreme

sure
   surer
   surest
surf *(ocean waves)*
   [serf *(feudal servant)*]
surface
   surfaced
   surfacing
surprise
   surprised
   surprising
surround
survey
   surveyor
survive
   survival
   survived
   surviving
   survivor
suspect

SW

swallow
swam
swamp
swang
swear *(irreg. vb.)*
sweat
sweater
Sweden
   Swede
   Swedish
sweep *(irreg. vb.)*
sweet *(sugary)*
   [suite *(connected rooms)*]
   sweeten
swell
swept
swift
swim *(irreg. vb.)*
   swimmer
   swimming
swing *(irreg. vb.)*
switch
   switches
Switzerland
   Swiss
sword
swore
sworn
swum
swung

sy

syllable
   syllabication
symbol *(a sign)*
   [cymbal *(a percussion
   instrument)*]
sympathy
   sympathetic
   sympathetically
   sympathies
   sympathize
symphony
   symphonies
symptom
   symptomatic
synagogue
synonym
   synonymous
Syria
   Syrian
system
   systematic
   systematically

ta

table
tacks *(flat-headed nails)*
tag
   tagged
   tagging
tax *(money paid to
   government)*
tail *(animal's hind appendage)*
   [tale *(story)*]
tailor
take *(irreg. vb.)*
   taken
   taking

*The following regular endings are not in the word list and can be added to the root word without changes:
-ed, -er, -est, -ful, -ing, -less, -ly, -ness, and -s. Most exceptions and root changes are in the list.*

tale *(story)*
  [tail *(animal's hind appendage)*]
talk
tall
tank
tap
  tapped
  tapping
tape
  taped
  taping
taps *(bugle call)*
tar
tardy
target
tart
task
taste
  tasted
  taster
  tastier
  tastiest
  tasting
taught *(did teach)*
  [taut *(tight)*]
tax *(money paid to government)*
  [tacks *(flat-headed nails)*]
  taxes

te

tea *(a beverage)*
  [tee *(holder for golf balls)*]
  teas
  [tease *(mock)*]
teach *(irreg. vb.)*
  teaches
team *(crew)*
  [teem *(swarm)*]
tear *(water from eye)*
  [tier *(a row)*]
tear *(irreg. vb.)*
teaspoon
tease *(mock)*
  [teas *(beverages)*]
technical
technique
tee *(holder for golf balls)*
  [tea *(a hot drink)*]
teem *(swarm)*
  [team *(crew)*]
teenage
  teenager

teeth
teetotal
telecast
telecommunication
telegram
  telegrammed
  telegramming
telephone
  telephoned
  telephoning
telescope
  telescoped
  telescoping
televise
  televised
  televising
  television
tell *(irreg. vb.)*
temperament
  temperamental
temperature
temporary
  temporarily
temple
tempt
ten
  tenth
tenant
tend
tendency
  tendencies
tender
Tennessee
tense
  tensed
  tensing
tent
tenth
term
tern *(sea bird)*
  [turn *(rotate)*]
terrible
  terribly
terrific
territory
  territorial
  territories
terror
test
Texas
texture
  textured
  texturing

th

than *(comparing)*
  [then *(at that time)*]
thank
Thanksgiving
that
the
theater
  theatrical
thee
their *(belonging to them)*
  [there *(at that place)*]
  [they're *(they are)*]
  theirs *(belonging to them)*
  [there's *(there is)*]
them
theme
themselves
then *(at that time)*
  [than *(comparing)*]
theory
there *(at that place)*
  [their *(belonging to them)*]
  [they're *(they are)*]
  there's *(there is)*
  [theirs *(belonging to them)*]
therefore
thermometer
thermonuclear
these
they
they'd *(they would)*
they'll *(they will)*
they're *(they are)*
  their *(belonging to them)*
  there *(at that place)*
thick
thief

thin
  thinned
  thinner
  thinnest
  thinning
thing
think *(irreg. vb.)*
third
thirsty
thirteen
  thirteenth
thirty
  thirties
  thirtieth
this
thorough
those
thou
though
thought
thousand
  thousandfold
  thousandth
thread
threat
three
threw *(tossed)*
  [through *(finished)*]
thrill
throat
throne *(ruler's chair)*
  [thrown *(tossed)*]
through *(finished)*
  [threw *(tossed)*]
throughout
throw *(irreg. vb.)*
  thrown *(tossed)*
  [throne *(ruler's chair)*]
thrust
thumb
thunder
Thursday
thus
thy
thyme *(herb)*
  time *(past, present, and future)*

ti

tic *(twitch)*
  [tick *(1. insect, 2. clock sound)*]
ticket
tickle
  tickled
  tickling
tide *(ebb and flow)*
  [tied *(bound)*]
tie
  tied *(bound)*
  [tide *(ebb and flow)*]
  tying
tier *(a row)*
  [tear *(water from eye)*]
tiger
tight
till
timber
time *(past, present, and future)*
  [thyme *(herb)*]
  timed
  timelier
  timeliest
  timeliness
  timely
  timer
  timing
timetable
timeworn
timid
  timidity
tin
  tinned
  tinning
tinder
tinderbox
tinfoil
tinge
  tinged
tiny
  tinier
  tiniest
tip
  tipped
  tipper
  tipping

tire
  tired
  tiredness
  tiring
tiresome
tissue
title
  titled
  titling

to

to *(toward)*
  [too *(also)*]
  [two *(the number 2)*]
toad *(frog-like animal)*
  [towed *(pulled)*]
tobacco
today
toe *(digit on foot)*
  [tow *(pull)*]
together
told *(informed)*
  [tolled *(rang)*]
tolled *(see told)*
tomorrow
ton
tone
tongue
  tongued
  tonguing
tonic
tonight
too *(also)*
  [to *(toward)*]
  [two *(the number 2)*]
took
tool
tooth
top
  topped
  topper
  topping
topic
  topical
topple
  toppled
  toppling
tore
torn

The following regular endings are not in the word list and can be added to the root word without changes: -ed, -er, -est, -ful, -ing, -less, -ly, -ness, and -s. Most exceptions and root changes are in the list.

torture
  tortured
  torturer
  torturing
toss
  tosses
total
touch
  touches
  touchier
  touchiest
  touchy
tough
tow *(pull)*
  [toe *(digit on foot)*]
  towed *(pulled)*
  [toad *(frog-like animal)*]
toward
tower
town
township
townspeople
toxic
  toxicity
toy

tr

trace
  traced
  tracer
  tracing
track
trade
  traded
  trader
  trading
tradition
  traditional
traffic
tragedy
  tragedies
tragic
  tragically
trail
train
transact
transatlantic
transform
translate
  translated
  translating
  translation
  translator

transportation
trap
  trapped
  trapper
  trapping
travel
tray
treasure
  treasured
  treasurer
  treasuring
treat
treatment
treaty
  treaties
tree
  treed
treelike
treetop
tremendous
trial
triangle
tribe
trick
  trickery
  tricky
tried
trim
  trimmed
  trimmer
  trimming
trip
  tripped
  tripping
troop *(military)*
  [troupe *(military)*]
tropical
trouble
  troubled
  troublesome
  troubling
troupe *(acting)*
  [troop *(acting)*]
truck
true
  truer
  truest
  truly
trumpet
trunk
trust *(confidence)*
  [trussed *(tied up)*]
truth

try
  tried
  tries

tu

tub
tube
Tuesday
tug
tumble
tune
  tuned
  tuning
tunnel
turkey *(bird)*
Turkey *(country)*
  Turkish
turn *(rotate)*
  [tern *(sea bird)*]
turtle

tw

twelve
  twelfth
twenty
  twenties
  twentieth
twice
twin
twist
two *(the number 2)*
  [to *(toward)*]
  [too *(also)*]

ty

type
  typed
  typing
typical

ug

ugly
  uglier
  ugliest
  ugliness

ul

ultimate

um
umbrella

un
unable
uncle
underground
underline
  underlined
  underlining
underneath
understand *(irreg. vb.)*
underwater
unexpected
unhappy
  unhappiest
  unhappily
  unhappiness
uniform
  uniformity
union
unique
unit
unite
  united
  uniting
United States
unity
universe
  universal
  universality
university
  universities
unkind
unknown
unless
unlike
unload
unlucky
unnecessary
unofficial
unrest
until
unusual
unwind *(irreg. vb.)*

up
up
upbeat
upbringing

upcoming
update
upend
upheaval
upholster
upon
upper
upright
upset
  upsetting
upstairs
upward

ur
uranium
urge
  urged
  urging
urgent
urn *(vase)*
  [earn *(work for)*]
Uruguay
  Uruguayan

us
us
use
  usage
  used
  using
usual

ut
Utah

va
vacant
vacation
vacuum
vague
vain *(conceited)*
  [vane *(wind indicator)*]
  [vein *(blood vessel)*]
vale *(valley)*
  [veil *(face covering)*]
vary *(change)*
  [very *(greatly)*]

ve
veil *(face covering)*
  [vale *(valley)*]
vein *(blood vessel)*
  [vain *(conceited)*]
  [vane *(wind indicator)*]
Venezuela
  Venezuelan
Venus
verb
  verbal
  verbalize
  verbalized
  verbalizing
Vermont
verse
  versed
version
versus
vertical
very *(greatly)*
  [vary *(change)*]
vessel

vi
vial *(jar)*
  [vile *(bad)*]
vibrate
  vibrated
  vibrating
  vibration
vice *(bad habit)*
  [vise *(a clamp)*]
victim
victory
  victories
  victorious
view
vile *(bad)*
  [vial *(jar)*]
village
  villager

The following regular endings are not in the word list and can be added to the root word without changes:
-ed, -er, -est, -ful, -ing, -less, -ly, -ness, and -s. Most exceptions and root changes are in the list.

villain
violate
  violated
  violating
  violation
violent
  violence
violet
violin
virgin
Virginia
  Virginian
vise *(a clamp)*
  [vice *(bad habit)*]
visible
  visibly
vision
  visionary
visit
  visitor
vitamin

vo

vocabulary
  vocabularies
vocation
voice
  voiced
  voicing
volcano
  volcanoes
volume
volunteer
  voluntary
vote
  voted
  voter
  voting
vowel
voyage
  voyaged
  voyager
  voyaging

wa

wade *(walk in water)*
  [weighed *(measured heaviness)*]
wage
  waged
  waging
wagon
wail *(cry)*
  [whale *(sea mammal)*]

waist *(middle of body)*
  [waste *(unused parts)*]
wait *(linger)*
  [weight *(heaviness)*]
waiter
waitress
waive *(give up rights)*
  [wave *(signal hello or good-bye)*]
wake
  waked
  waken
  waking
walk
wall
wander
want *(desire)*
  [wont *(custom)*]
war
  warrior
ware *(pottery)*
  [wear *(have on body)*]
  [where *(what place)*]
warm
  warmth
warn
was
wash
  washes
Washington
  Washingtonian
wasn't *(was not)*
waste *(unused parts)*
  [waist *(middle of body)*]
  wasted
  wasting
watch
  watches
water
wave *(signal hello or good-bye)*
  [waive *(give up rights)*]
  waved
  waving
wax
  waxes
way *(road)*
  [weigh *(measure heaviness)*]
  [whey *(watery part of milk)*]

we

we *(us)*
  [wee *(small)*]
wear *(have on body) (irreg. vb.)*
  [ware *(pottery)*]
  [where *(what place)*]
weather *(climate)*
  [whether *(if)*]
weave *(interlace) (irreg. vb.)*
  [we've *(we have)*]
Wednesday
weed *(a plant)*
  [we'd *(we would)*]
week *(seven days)*
  [weak *(not strong)*]
weekend
weep *(irreg. vb.)*
weigh *(measure heaviness)*
  [way *(road)*]
  [whey *(watery part of milk)*]
  weighed *(measured heaviness)*
  [wade *(walk in water)*]
weight *(heaviness)*
  [wait *(linger)*]
weir *(dam)*
  [we're *(we are)*]
welcome
  welcomed
  welcoming
well
we'll *(we will)*
  [weal *(well-being)*]
  [wheel *(circular frame)*]
went
wept
were
we're *(we are)*
  [weir *(dam)*]
weren't *(were not)*
west *(direction)*
  western
  westward
West *(geographical area)*
West Virginia

wet *(moist) (irreg. vb.)*
  [whet *(sharpen)*]
  wetted
  wetter
  wettest
  wetting
we've *(we have)*
  [weave *(interlace)*]

wh

whale *(sea mammal)*
  [wail *(cry)*]
  whaling
what
whatever
wheat
wheel *(circular frame)*
  [weal *(well-being)*]
  [we'll *(we will)*]
when
whenever
where *(what place)*
  [ware *(pottery)*]
  [wear *(have on body)*]
  wherever
whet *(sharpen)*
  [wet *(moist)*]
whether *(if)*
  [weather *(climate)*]
whey *(watery part of milk)*
  [way *(road)*]
  [weigh *(measure heaviness)*]
which *(what one)*
  [witch *(sorceress)*]
while *(during)*
  [wile *(a trick)*]
whine *(complain)*
  [wine *(a drink)*]
whip
  whipped
  whipping
whisper
whistle
  whistled
  whistling
white
  whited
  whiten
  whiter
  whitest

whitewash
whiz
  whizzed
  whizzing
who
whoever
whole *(complete)*
  [hole *(an opening)*]
  wholly *(completely)*
  [holey *(full of holes)*]
  [holy *(sacred)*]
whom
who's *(who is)*
  [whose *(who owns)*]
whose *(see who's)*
why

wi

wicked
wide
  widen
  wider
  widest
  width
wife
  wives
wild
wilderness
wile *(a trick)*
  [while *(during)*]
will
win
  winner
  winning
wind *(irreg. vb.)*
window
wine *(a drink)*
  [whine *(complain)*]
wing
wink
winter
wipe
  wiped
  wiper
  wiping
wire
  wired
  wiring
Wisconsin

wise
  wiser
  wisest
wish
  wishes
wit
  wittier
  wittiest
  wittily
  wittiness
  wittingly
  witty
witch *(sorceress)*
  [which *(what one)*]
  witches
with
withdraw
  withdrawal
  withdrawn
withhold
within
without
withstand
witness
wizard
  wizardry

wo

wobble
  wobbled
  wobbling
woe
woebegone
woke
wolf
  wolfish
  wolves
woman
  women
won *(triumphed)*
  [one *(the number 1)*]
wonder
  wondrous

The following regular endings are not in the word list and can be added to the root word without changes:
-ed, -er, -est, -ful, -ing, -less, -ly, -ness, and -s. Most exceptions and root changes are in the list.

wonderland
wont *(custom)*
   [want *(desire)*]
won't *(would not)*
wood *(of a tree)*
   [would *(is willing to)*]
   woodsy
woodchuck
woodland
woodpile
woodshed
woodwork
wool
   woolen
   woolier
   woolliest
word
   wordier
   wordiest
   wordy
wore
work
   workable
workshop
world
   worldlier
   worldliest
   worldliness
   wordly
worm
worn
worry
   worried
   worrier
worse
   worsen
worship
   worshipped
   worshipper
   worshipping
worst *(most bad)*
   [wurst *(sausage)*]
worth
   worthy
worthwhile
would *(is willing to)*
   [wood *(of a tree)*]
wouldn't *(would not)*
wound
wove
   woven

wr

wrap *(cover)*
   [rap *(hit)*]
   wrapped
   wrapping
wreak *(inflict)*
   [reek *(give off strong odor)*]
wreck

wrench
   wrenches
wrest *(take from)*
   [rest *(relax)*]
wring *(squeeze) (irreg. vb.)*
   [ring *(circular band)*]
write *(inscribe) (irreg. vb.)*
   [right *(correct)*]
   [rite *(ceremony)*]
   writer
   writing
   written
wrong
wrote *(did write)*
   [rote *(by memory)*]
wrung *(squeezed)*
   [rung *(a step on a ladder)*]
wurst *(sausage)*
   [worst *(most bad)*]
wry *(ironically humorous)*
   [rye *(grain)*]
Wyoming

xr

x-ray

xy

xylophone

ya

yacht
yard
yarn

ye

year
yell
yellow
   yellowish
yelp
yes
   yeses
yesterday
yesteryear
yet
yew *(a shrub)*
   [ewe *(female sheep)*]
   [you *(yourself)*]

yo

yoke *(harness)*
   [yolk *(egg center)*]
you *(yourself)*
   [ewe *(female sheep)*]
   [yew *(a shrub)*]

you'd *(you would)*
you'll *(you will)*
   [yule *(Christmas)*]
young
your *(belonging to you)*
   [you're *(you are)*]
you're *(you are)*
   [your *(belonging to you)*]
yourself
youth
you've *(you have)*

yu

Yugoslavia
   Yugoslavian
yule *(Christmas)*
   [you'll *(you will)*]

ze
zeal
    zealous
zebra
zero
    zeroed
    zeroes
    zeroing
zest

zi
zip
    zipped
    zipping
zipper

zo
zone
    zoned
    zoning
zoo
zookeeper
zoology

The following regular endings are not in the word list and can be added to the root word without changes:
-ed, -er, -est, -ful, -ing, -less, -ly, -ness, and -s. Most exceptions and root changes are in the list.

PERSONAL SPELLING LIST

A lot of writers keep a "Personal Spelling List." This list is made up of:

1. Words that they have to look up in a dictionary.
2. Words that they frequently misspell.
3. Names of people, cities, and things not easily found in a dictionary or spelling list.
4. Words unique to a subject (like biology, music, or sports).
5. Foreign words and phrases.

Writing the word in a personal list helps a writer learn the correct spelling of the word and is much faster and easier way to find than in a dictionary.

A _____   _____   _____

_____   _____   _____

_____   _____   _____

_____   _____   _____

B _____   _____   _____

_____   _____   _____

_____   _____   _____

_____   _____   _____

C _____   _____   _____

_____   _____   _____

_____   _____   _____

D

E

F

G

H

I

J

K

L

M

N

O

P

_____   _____   _____

_____   _____   _____

Q

_____   _____   _____

_____   _____   _____

R

_____   _____   _____

_____   _____   _____

_____   _____   _____

_____   _____   _____

S

_____   _____   _____

_____   _____   _____

_____   _____   _____

_____   _____   _____

_____   _____   _____

_____   _____   _____

T

_____ _____ _____

_____ _____ _____

_____ _____ _____

_____ _____ _____

_____ _____ _____

U

_____ _____ _____

_____ _____ _____

_____ _____ _____

V

_____ _____ _____

_____ _____ _____

_____ _____ _____

W

_____ _____ _____

_____ _____ _____

_____ _____ _____

_____ _____ _____

_____ _____ _____

X

Y

Z

SPELLING RULES

Here are a few basic spelling rules.

Plurals and "S" Forms of Verbs

1. Add "s" to most nouns and verbs.
   Examples: ants, cowboys, runs

2. Add "es" if the word ends in "ch," "s," "sh," "x," or "z."
   Examples: box - boxes, church - churches, wash - washes

3. For words ending in "f" or "fe":
   a. If the final "f" sound is still heard in the plural form, add an "s."
      Examples: chief - chiefs, roof - roofs
   b. If a final "v" sound is heard in the plural form, change the "f" to "v" and add "es."
      Examples: leaf - leaves, wife - wives

4. For words ending in "o":
   a. If preceded by a vowel, add an "s."
      Examples: radio - radios, studio - studios
   b. If preceded by a consonant, add "es."
      Example: go - goes
   c. If a musical term, add "s."
      Examples: piano - pianos, solo - solos

5. For words ending in "y":
   a. If preceded by a vowel, add an "s."
      Examples: monkey - monkeys, toy - toys
   b. If preceded by a consonant, change the "y" to "i" and add "es."
      Examples: baby - babies, city - cities
   c. If a proper noun, add "s."
      Example: one Kathy - two Kathys

Other Plurals

1. Some foreign nouns have different plurals.
   Examples: alumnus - alumni, index - indices

2. A few nouns have irregular plurals.
   Examples: foot - feet, child - children, woman - women

3. A few nouns don't change for plurals.
   Example: deer - deer

4. Plurals of compound nouns are often formed by adding "s" or "es" to the important word.
   Example: brother-in-law - brothers-in-law
5. The plural form of symbols often use an apostrophe.
   Examples: 2's, ABC's

"EI" and "IE" Rule

It is often difficult to remember whether a word is spelled with an "ei" or an "ie." Here are some basic rules to help.

1. If the vowel has a long "a" sound, spell it "ei."
   Examples: neighbor, weigh
2. Write "i" before "e," except after "c."
   Examples: chief, believe
3. There are plenty of exceptions to these rules.
   Examples: their, Neil, science, either, leisure

Compound Words

A compound word is two words put together to form a new word.
Basic Rule: Keep the full spelling of each word. Do not use a hyphen.
   Examples: ear + ring = earring, room + mate = roommate
A more common usage or more specific meaning tends to put two words into a compound.
   Examples: blackbird (one word), black car (two words)

The following are some commonly-used compound words.

airplane	fireplace	playmate
backyard	flashlight	popcorn
baseball	football	roommate
basketball	girlfriend	skateboard
bathroom	hairbrush	softball
blackboard	haircut	sunglasses
boyfriend	nightlight	tablecloth
campfire	pancake	toothbrush
cowboy	pillowcase	washcloth

PREFIXES

Prefixes are added onto the front of a word and often change the meaning of the word.

Examples: un + happy = unhappy, hyper + active = hyperactive

Basic Rule: A prefix is added to the front of a word and does not change the spelling.

1. Even if it means having double letters.
   Examples: mis + spell = misspell
   il + legible = illegible

2. The prefixes "ex" and "self" are often used with a hyphen.
   Examples: ex-resident, self-help

Here are a few of the most common prefixes, their meanings, and sample words:

Prefixes	Definitions	Examples
dis-	not, apart	disobey
em-, en-	in, into	empower, enslave
im-, in-	into	impossible, inside
inter-	between	intertwine
intro-	into, inward	introvert
mis-	bad, incorrect	misjudged
non-	not	nonsense
over-	excessive	overpower
pre-	before	prehistoric
re-	again, back	return
sub-	under	submarine
un-	not	unhappy

SUFFIXES

Suffixes are added at the end of a word. The most common suffix endings include: -ed, -er, -est, -ful, -ing, -less, -ly, -ness, and -s.

Basic Rule: Just add the suffix (except as noted under "Exceptions"). Adding most suffixes does not change the spelling.

Examples: rest + ed = rested, rest + ful = restful, rest + ing = resting, rest + less = restless, rest + s = rests

Exceptions:

1. For words ending in "c":
   a. Add a "k" before any suffix that begins with an "e," "i," or "y."
      Example: picnic - picnicking, panic - panicky

SUFFIXES *(cont.)*

2. For words ending in "e":
   a. Drop the final "e" if the suffix begins with a vowel.
      Examples: rose - rosy, name - named - naming

   b. Keep the final "e" if the suffix begins with a consonant.
      Example: safe - safely

   c. Keep the final "e" if a vowel preceded it.
      Example: see - seeing

   d. Drop the final "le" if the suffix is "ly" (no double "l").
      Example: able - ably

3. For words ending in "y":
   a. Just add the suffix if the "y" is preceded by a vowel.
      Examples: joy - joyful, joyless, joyous

   b. Change the "y" to "i" if it is preceded by a consonant.
      Examples: carry - carried, history - historic

   c. Do not change the "y" to "i" if the suffix begins with an "i."
      Example: carry - carrying

4. Double the final consonant before adding the suffix if:
   a. The word has one syllable (or the final syllable is accented).
   b. The word ends in a single consonant (but not "x").
   c. The word has a single vowel letter.
   d. The suffix begins with a vowel.
      Example: brag - bragged (not "x," box - boxing)

   e. The word has two syllables and is accented on the last syllable.
      Example: admit - admittance

   f. A word ends in "l" and the suffix being added is "ly" (even though it looks odd with two "l's").
      Example: cool - coolly

5. Do not double the final consonant if:
   a. The suffix begins with a consonant.
      Example: bag - bagful
   b. The vowel has two letters.
      Example: rain - rained
   c. The word has two final consonant.
      Example: hard - harder
   d. The final syllable is not accented.
      Example: benefit - benefited
   e. If the word has two syllables and is accented on the first syllable.
      Example: equal - equaled

SPELLING USING PHONICS

Phonics rules are useful in learning to read because students learn to sound out unknown or unfamiliar words. Phonics is also important in learning to spell because the sound-letter (phoneme-grapheme) correspondence works both ways. Unfortunately, phonics isn't perfect. There are many exceptions or variations on sound-letter correspondence, but there are also plenty of words and parts of words that are spelled regularly.

The following two phonics charts for vowels and consonants can help writers learn to spell many words and parts of words correctly. In fact, the letter-sound correspondences in these charts are a set of spelling rules based on phonics. Young children use invented spelling, which is actually a kind of spatial knowledge of phonics. As children get older (or writers mature), they still use invented spelling sometimes, but their invented spelling is better because they know more phonics, plus they have learned the spelling of many letter clusters.

The following charts can also help in looking up words in the "Spelling Checklist." If a student can sound out a word (know the phonemes), then he or she can look up the common and less common spellings in the charts.

All vowels and some consonants have more than one way to be spelled. Three consonant letters (c, q, and x) have no sound (phoneme) of their own. The letter "c" makes either a /k/ sound (as in "cat") or an /s/ sound (as in "city"). The letter "c" generally makes the /s/ sound before an "i," "e," and "y"; it makes the /k/ sound before "a," "o," and "u." The letter "q" always appears with a "u," and "qu" makes the /kw/ sound (as in "queen"). The letter "x" usually makes the /ks/ sound (as in "box").

The consonants "g" and "s" have more than one sound. The letter "g" can sound like a /g/ (as in "girl") or a /j/ (as in "gem"). The letter "s" can make an /s/ sound (as in "see") or a /z/ sound (as in "is"). The letter "s" makes the /z/ sound only at the end of some words. The digraph "th" has two sounds: voiced (as in "them") and unvoiced (as in "thin").

The letter "y" acts as a consonant at the beginning of most words (as in "yesterday") and a vowel in the middle or end of a word (as in "cycle" or "funny"). See the "Vowel Exceptions" section in the phonics charts.

SPELLING USING PHONICS *(cont.)*

Most linguists and dictionaries say that the digraph "wh" really represents the /hw/ blend, but this is a highly technical point of little concern (or interest) to most persons. The same is true for the digraph "ng," which is a unique /ng/ phoneme.

The schwa is an unaccented vowel sound that is very much like a short "u." It is helpful to remember that to have an unaccented vowel the word must also have at least one other accented vowel sound. Some consonant sounds should be pronounced in isolation without a schwa (uh) sound. For example, the letter "b" needs a schwa and is pronounced "buh," but the letter "f" is simply the "fff" sound of air rushing past the teeth without vocal chords being used.

A blend is two different phonemes that occur together so that each is sounded, for example the "bl" as in "black." This is different from a consonant digraph like "sh," which makes its own phoneme and is not a blend of /s/ and /h/. A list of the digraphs are in the phonics charts.

Of course, there are plenty of exceptions to the number of phonics presented in the vowel and consonant charts. That is why you have to learn to spell many words by "sight" or the whole word approach. It is also why the "Spelling Checklist" should be a consonant companion when writing anything. For additional help with spelling, see the *Spelling Book* listed on the inside back cover.

VOWEL SOUNDS: ALPHABETICAL

Phoneme		Common Spelling	Less Common Spelling
A Short	ă	A hat	
A Long	ā	A-E age, aid	EIGH eight, AY say, A (R) vary, AI (R) fair
A Broad	ä	A (R) far	A father
E Short	ě	E red	EA head
E Long	ē	E repay, EE see	EA seat, Y crazy
I Short	ĭ	I bit	Y gym
I Long	ī	I-E ice, Y try, I child	
O Short	ŏ	O hot	A watch
O Long	ō	O so, O-E nose	OA boat, OW know
O Broad	ô	O (R) for	A (L) all, A (U) auto A (W) awful
OI + OY	oy	OI boil, OY boy	
OU + OW	ou	OU out, OW owl	U ruby, EW chew
OO Long	o͞o, ü	OO moon	U (L) pull, playful
OO Short	o͝o, u̇	OO good	
U Short	ŭ	U nut	
U Long	ū	U-E use, U music	
∂ Schwa	∂	A alone, E taken, I direct, OU generous	
		O riot, U campus	
		(Note: The schwa phoneme is the unaccented vowel sound so it must be a polysyllabic word.)	

VOWEL SOUNDS: CLUSTERED

Short Vowels

a - at	/ ă /
e - end	/ ĕ /
i - is	/ ĭ /
o - hot	/ ŏ /
u - up	/ ŭ /

Long Vowel
Digraphs

ai - aid	/ ā /
ay - say	/ ā /
ea - eat	/ ē /
ee - see	/ ē /
oa - oat	/ ō /
ow - own	/ ō /

Dipthongs

oi - oil	/ oi /
oy - boy	/ oi /
ou - out	/ ou /
ow - how	/ ou /

Long Vowels
Open Syllable Rule

a - baby	/ ā /
e - we	/ ē /
i - idea	/ ī /
o - so	/ ō /

Schwa

u - hurt	/ ∂ /
e - happen	/ ∂ /
o - other	/ ∂ /

Vowel Y

y - try	/ ī /
y - funny	/ ē /

Double O

oo - soon	/ o͞o /
oo - good	/ o͝o /
u - truth	/ o͞o /
u - put	/ o͝o /

Long Vowels
Final E Rule

a - make	/ ā /
e - here	/ ē /
i - five	/ ī /
o - home	/ ō /
u - use	/ ū /

Vowel Plus R

er - her	/ r /
ir - sir	/ r /
ur - fur	/ r /
ar - far	/ är /
ar - vary	/ ār /
or - for	/ ôr /

Broad O

o - long	/ ô /
a(l) - also	/ ô /
a(w) - saw	/ ô /
a(u) - auto	/ ô /

Vowel Exceptions

ea - bread	/ ē /	"ea" makes both a long and a short E sound.
e (silent) - come		E at the end of a word is usually silent and sometimes makes the preceding vowel long.
y - yes	/ y /	y is a consonant at the beginning of a word. (yes) y is long I in a one-syllable word or middle. (cycle) y is long E at the end of a polysyllable word. (funny)
al - pedal	/ ∂l /	Final AL makes a schwa plus L sound.
le - candle	/ ∂l /	Final LE makes a schwa plus L sound.
ul - awful	/ ∂l /	Final UL makes a schwa plus L sound.

CONSONANT SOUNDS: ALPHABETICAL

Phoneme	Common Spelling	Less Common Spelling
B	B boy	
C	(No "C" phoneme; see K and S)	
CH	CH cheese	T nature
D	D dog	
F	F fat	PH phone
G	G girl	
H	H hot	
J	J just, G giant	
K	C cat, K king	CK sick, CH chrome
KS	X fox (No "X" phoneme)	
KW	QU quick (No "Q" phoneme)	
L	L look	
M	M me	
N	N no	KN knife
NG	NG sing	
P	P put	
Q	(No "Q" phoneme; see KW)	
R	R run	WR write
S	S sit, C city	
SH	SH shut, TI action	
T	T toy	
TH (voiced)	TH this	
TH (voiceless)	TH thing	
V	V voice	
W	W will	
WH	WH white	
X	(No "X" phoneme; see KS)	
Y (consonant)	Y yes	I onion
Z	S is, Z zero	
ZH	SI vision	S pleasure

CONSONANT SOUNDS: CLUSTERED

Single Consonants

b	c	d	f
g	h	j	k
l	m	n	p
r	s	t	v
w	y	z	

Important Exceptions

c = /k/ before a, o, or u, as in "cat"
c = /s/ before i, e, or y as in "city"
g = /g/ before a, o, or s, as in "good"
g = /j/ before i, e, or y, as in "gem"
ng = /ng/ unique phoneme, as in "sing"
ph = /f/ sound, as in "phone"
qu = /kw/ blend, as in "quick"
    (the letter "q" is never used without "u")
s = /z/ sound at the end of some words, as in "is"
x = /ks/ blend, as in "fox"

Consonant Digraphs

ch as in "church"
sh as in "shoe"
th (voiced) as in "thin"
th (voiceless) as in "this"
wh (hw blend) as in "which"

Rare Exceptions

ch = /k/ as in "character"
ch = /sh/ as in "chef"
s = /sh/ as in "sure"
s = /zh/ as in "measure"
si = /zh/ as in "vision"
ti = /sh/ as in "attention"
x = /gz/ as in "exact"

Silent Consonants

ck = /k/ as in "back"
gh = /-/ as in "right"
gn = /n/ as in "gnat"
kn = /n/ as in "knife"
lf = /f/ as in "calf"
lk = /k/ as in "walk"
mb = /m/ as in "lamb"
tle = /l/ as in "castle"
wr = /r/ as in "write"

Beginning Consonant Blends

L family	*R family*	*S family*	*3-letter family*	*No family*
bl	br	sc	sch	dw
cl	cr	sk	scr	tw
fl	dr	sm	shr	
gl	fr	sn	spl	
pl	gr	sp	spr	
sl	pr	st	squ	
	tr	sw	str	
	wr		thr	

Final Consonant Blends

ct - act	**lt** - salt	**nd** - and	**pt** - kept	**rt** - art
ft - lift	**mp** - jump	**nk** - ink	**rd** - hard	**sk** - risk
ld - old	**nc** (e) - since	**nt** - ant	**rk** - dark	**st** - least

ABBREVIATIONS

U.S. Post Office State Abbreviations

(Note: No periods are used.)

State	Abbr.	State	Abbr.
Alabama	AL	Montana	MT
Alaska	AK	Nebraska	NE
Arizona	AZ	Nevada	NV
Arkansas	AR	New Hampshire	NH
California	CA	New Jersey	NJ
Colorado	CO	New Mexico	NM
Connecticut	CT	New York	NY
Delaware	DE	North Carolina	NC
District of Columbia	DC	North Dakota	ND
Florida	FL	Ohio	OH
Georgia	GA	Oklahoma	OK
Hawaii	HI	Oregon	OR
Idaho	ID	Pennsylvania	PA
Illinois	IL	Rhode Island	RI
Indiana	IN	South Carolina	SC
Iowa	IA	South Dakota	SD
Kansas	KS	Tennessee	TN
Kentucky	KY	Texas	TX
Louisiana	LA	Utah	UT
Maine	ME	Vermont	VT
Maryland	MD	Virginia	VA
Massachusetts	MA	Washington	WA
Michigan	MI	West Virginia	WV
Minnesota	MN	Wisconsin	WI
Mississippi	MS	Wyoming	WY
Missouri	MO		

ABBREVIATIONS *(cont.)*

Street Abbreviations

Alley . . . . Aly.

Arcade . . . . Arc.

Boulevard . . . . Blvd.

Branch . . . . Br.

Bypass . . . . Byp.

Causeway . . . . Cswy.

Center . . . . Ctr.

Circle . . . . Cir.

Court . . . . Ct.

Courts . . . . Cts.

Crescent . . . . Cres.

Drive . . . . Dr.

Expressway . . . . Expy.

Extended . . . . Ext.

Extension . . . . Ext.

Freeway . . . . Fwy.

Gardens . . . . Gdns.

Heights . . . . Hts.

Highway . . . . Hwy.

Lane . . . . Ln.

Manor . . . . Mnr.

Place . . . . Pl.

Plaza . . . . Plz.

Point . . . . Pt.

Road . . . . Rd.

Rural . . . . R.

Square . . . . Sq.

Street . . . . St.

Terrace . . . . Ter.

Trail . . . . Trl.

Turnpike . . . . Tpke.

Viaduct . . . . Via.

Vista . . . . Vis.

ABBREVIATIONS *(cont.)*

Titles

Doctor . . . . Dr.

Father . . . . Fr.

Governor . . . . Gov.

Honorable (judge) . . . . Hon.

Mister . . . . Mr.

President . . . . Pres.

Representative . . . . Rep.

Reverend . . . . Rev.

Senator . . . . Sen.

Vice President . . . . V.P.

Woman . . . . Ms.

Woman - married . . . . Mrs.

Woman - unmarried . . . . Miss

Time

Minute . . . . min.

Second . . . . sec.

After noon . . . . P.M. or p.m.
(post meridian)

Before noon . . . . A.M. or a.m.
(ante meridian)

Central Daylight Time . . . . CDT

Central Standard Time . . . . CST

Eastern Daylight Time . . . . EDT

Eastern Standard Time . . . . EST

Greenwich Mean Time . . . . GMT

Mountain Daylight Time . . . . MDT

Mountain Standard Time . . . . MST

Pacific Daylight Time . . . . PDT

Pacific Standard Time . . . . PST

ABBREVIATIONS *(cont.)*

Scholarly Degrees

Bachelor of Arts. . . . . B.A.

Bachelor of Science . . . . B.S.

Certified Public Accountant . . . . C.P.A.

Doctor of Dental Surgery . . . . D.D.S.

Doctor of Medicine . . . . M.D.

Doctor of Philosophy . . . . Ph.D.

Master of Arts . . . . M.A.

Months

January . . . . Jan.

February . . . . Feb.

March . . . . Mar.

April . . . . Apr.

May . . . . May

June . . . . Jun.

July . . . . July

August . . . . Aug.

September . . . . Sept.

October . . . . Oct.

November . . . . Nov.

December . . . . Dec.

Days of the Week

Sunday. . . . . Sun.

Monday . . . . Mon.

Tuesday . . . . Tue.

Wednesday . . . . Wed.

Thursday . . . . Thurs.

Friday . . . . Fri.

Saturday . . . . Sat.

ABBREVIATIONS *(cont.)*

Standard (U.S.) Measurements
(Note: Use a period.)

Capacity - dry

pint . . . . pt.
quart . . . . qt.
peck. . . . . pk.
bushel . . . . bu.

Capacity - liquid

ounce. . . . . oz.
pint . . . . pt.
quart . . . . qt.
gallon . . . . gal.
barrell . . . . bbl.

Length

foot . . . . ft.
furlong. . . . . fur.
inch . . . . in.
mile. . . . . mi.
rod. . . . . r.
yard. . . . . yd.

Temperature

Fahrenheit . . . . F

Weight

dram . . . . dr.
ounce. . . . . oz.
pound . . . . lb.
hundredweight. . . . . hwt.
ton. . . . . t.

ABBREVIATIONS *(cont.)*

Metric Measurements

(Note: Do not use a period.)

Capacity

milliliter . . . . ml
centiliter cl
deciliter . . . . dl
liter l
decaliter . . . . dk
hectoliter . . . . h
kiloliter . . . . k

Length

millimeter . . . . mm
centimeter . . . . cm
decimeter . . . . dm
meter . . . . m
decameter . . . . dkm
hectometer . . . . hm
kilometer . . . . km

Temperature

centigrade C
Celsius C

Weight

milligram . . . . mg
centigram . . . . cg
decigram . . . . dg
gram . . . . g
decagram . . . . dkg
hectogram . . . . hg
kilogram . . . . kg

ABBREVIATIONS *(cont.)*

Parts of Speech

(For an explanation of "Parts of Speech," see page 98.)

adjectives . . . . adj.

adverb . . . . adv.

conjunction. . . . . conj.

interjection . . . . inter.

noun . . . . n.

preposition . . . . prep.

pronoun . . . . pron.

verb . . . . vb.

Common Reference Abbreviations

continued . . . . cont.

et cetera (Latin for "and so forth") . . . . etc.
    (pronounced et-SET-uh-ruh)

example . . . . ex., e.g., or Ex.

id est (Latin for "that is") . . . . i.e.

miscellaneous. . . . . misc.

page . . . . p.

pages . . . . pp.

post postscriptum
    (Latin for "a later postscript"). . . . . P.P.S.

postscriptum (Latin for "postscript") . . . . P.S.

volume . . . . vol.

STUDYING FOR SPELLING

Learning how to spell words is important. It helps you become a better writer and also makes writing easier. Here is a simple and effective method that can aid you in becoming a better speller.

5-Step Spelling Word Study Method for Students

1. **Look** at the whole word carefully.

2. **Say** the word aloud to yourself.

3. **Spell** the word. Say each letter to yourself.

4. **Write** the word from memory. Cover the word and write it.

5. **Check** your written word against the correct spelling. Circle errors, and repeat steps 4 and 5.

REFERENCES
State Capitals

Listed below are the 50 states that comprise the United States of America. Also listed are the state capitals, the date when each became a state, and the order in which the states entered the union. Our nation's capital is Washington, DC (District of Columbia).

State	Capital	Statehood	Order
Alabama	Montgomery	Dec. 14, 1819	22
Alaska	Juneau	Jan. 3, 1959	49
Arizona	Phoenix	Feb. 14, 1912	48
Arkansas	Little Rock	June 15, 1836	25
California	Sacramento	Sept. 9, 1850	31
Colorado	Denver	Aug. 1, 1876	38
Connecticut	Hartford	Jan. 9, 1788	5
Delaware	Dover	Dec. 7, 1787	1
Florida	Tallahassee	Mar. 3, 1845	27
Georgia	Atlanta	Jan. 2, 1788	4
Hawaii	Honolulu	Aug. 21, 1959	50
Idaho	Boise	July 3, 1890	43
Illinois	Springfield	Dec. 3, 1818	21
Indiana	Indianapolis	Dec. 11, 1816	19
Iowa	Des Moines	Dec. 28, 1846	29
Kansas	Topeka	Jan. 29, 1861	34
Kentucky	Frankfort	June 1, 1792	15
Louisiana	Baton Rouge	Apr. 30, 1812	18
Maine	Augusta	Mar. 15, 1820	23
Maryland	Annapolis	Apr. 28, 1788	7
Massachusetts	Boston	Feb. 6, 1788	6
Michigan	Lansing	Jan. 26, 1837	26
Minnesota	St. Paul	May 11, 1858	32

REFERENCES *(cont.)*

State Capitals

State	Capital	Statehood	Order
Mississippi	Jackson	Dec. 10, 1817	20
Missouri	Jefferson City	Aug. 10, 1821	24
Montana	Helena	Nov. 8, 1889	41
Nebraska	Lincoln	Mar. 1, 1867	37
Nevada	Carson City	Oct. 31, 1864	36
New Hampshire	Concord	June 21, 1788	9
New Jersey	Trenton	Dec. 18, 1787	3
New Mexico	Santa Fe	Jan. 6, 1912	47
New York	Albany	July 26, 1788	11
North Carolina	Raleigh	Nov. 21, 1789	12
North Dakota	Bismarck	Nov. 2, 1889	39
Ohio	Columbus	Mar. 1, 1803	17
Oklahoma	Oklahoma City	Nov. 16, 1907	46
Oregon	Salem	Feb. 14, 1859	33
Pennsylvania	Harrisburg	Dec. 12, 1787	2
Rhode Island	Providence	May 29, 1790	13
South Carolina	Columbia	May 23, 1788	8
South Dakota	Pierre	Nov. 2, 1889	40
Tennessee	Nashville	June 1, 1796	16
Texas	Austin	Dec. 29, 1845	28
Utah	Salt Lake City	Jan. 4, 1896	45
Vermont	Montpelier	Mar. 4, 1791	14
Virginia	Richmond	June 25, 1788	10
Washington	Olympia	Nov. 11, 1889	42
West Virginia	Charleston	June 20, 1863	35
Wisconsin	Madison	May 29, 1848	30
Wyoming	Cheyenne	July 10, 1890	44

REFERENCES *(cont.)*
Measurements

Sometimes when writing, measurements are included. This chart lists basic U.S. and metric units of measurement, plus gives information for converting from one unit to another.

Standard U.S. Units of Length
1 foot (ft.) = 12 inches (in.)
1 yard (yd.) = 3 feet = 36 inches
1 mile (mi.) = 1,760 yards = 5,280 feet
1 fathom (fath.) = 6 feet
1 nautical mile = 6,076.1 feet

Metric Units of Length
1000 millimeters (mm) = 1 meter
100 centimeters (cm) = 1 meter
1 centimeter = 10 millimeters
10 decimeters (dm) = 1 meter
1 decimeter = 10 centimeters
1 dekameter (dkm) = 10 meters
1 kilometer (km) = 1000 meters

Dry Measure
1 pint (pt.) = 16 ounces (oz.)
1 quart (qt.) = 2 pints = 32 ounces
1 peck = 8 quarts
1 bushel = 4 pecks

Conversion Factors for Units of Length
1 inch = 2.54 centimeters
1 foot = 0.305 meter
1 yard = 0.914
1 mile = 1.609 kilometers
1 nautical mile = 1.852 kilometers
1 centimeter = 0.39 inch
1 meter = 39.37 inches = 3.28 feet = 1.094 yards
1 kilometer = 0.62 mil

Temperature
Celsius = (5/9 x Fahrenheit) - 32
Fahrenheit = (9/5 x Celsius) + 32

Liquid Measure
1 cup (c.) = 8 ounces (oz.)
1 pint (pt.) = 16 fluid ounces
1 quart (qt.) = 2 pints = 32 ounces
1 gallon (gal.) = 4 quarts = 8 pints

REFERENCES *(cont.)*

Roman Numerals

Roman numerals are occasionally used when writing. Therefore, the following chart has been included to help writers learn to use them correctly. Since Roman numerals follow a consistent format, only the first 20 numerals (numbers 1-20) are given below, along with the larger numerals (20, 30, 40, etc.).

I	1	XVI	16
II	2	XVII	17
III	3	XVIII	18
IV	4	XIX	19
V	5	XX	20
VI	6	XXX	30
VII	7	XL	40
VIII	8	L	50
IX	9	LX	60
X	10	LXX	70
XI	11	LXXX	80
XII	12	XC	90
XIII	13	C	100
XIV	14	D	500
XV	15	M	1,000

PARTS OF SPEECH

To understand grammar, it is helpful to know about the parts of speech, which are a way of classifying words. There are eight basic types of words, which all writers need to know. (See also "Sentences: Basic Construction" on pages 100–102.)

1. **Noun** — The name of a person, place or thing. A simple test for a noun is: If you can put the word "the" or "a" in front of it, it is probably a noun. Note that every sentence must have a noun or pronoun.

   Examples: ball, hat, dog, man

   Proper nouns name a particular person, place, or thing. All proper nouns are capitalized.

   Examples: Mr. Smith, America, Fido

2. **Pronoun** — A word used in place of a noun. Every sentence must have a noun or pronoun.

   Examples: he, you, it, their, someone

3. **Adjective** — A word that describes a noun or pronoun. (See "Comparative Adjectives" on page 99.)

   Examples: green, big, all, those, some, beautiful

   There is a special kind of adjective called an article, and there are only three articles: "the," "a," and "an." An adjective can also be between the noun and the article.

   Example: the big box

4. **Verb** — A word that shows some kind of action or state. Every sentence must have a verb.

   Examples: run, study, read, is

5. **Adverb** — A word that describes a verb, adjective, or other adverb.

   Examples: quietly, fearfully, very, often, too

   Many adverbs end in "ly," and are formed by adding "ly" to an adjective.

   Examples: warm - warmly, beautiful - beautifully

6. **Conjunction** — A word used to join words or phrases.

   Examples: and, or, but, because

7. **Preposition** — A word used to show the relationship of a noun or pronoun to another word.

   Examples: of, form, above, at, to, with

   A preposition can be put in front of a noun (and its adjectives) to form a prepositional phrase, which then acts like an adjective or adverb. A prepositional phrase can modify the noun or pronoun, or it can modify a verb.

   Examples: Bill, <u>from Arkansas,</u> was the first choice. (adjective)

   Bill hit the ball <u>to Jose.</u> (adverb)

PARTS OF SPEECH *(cont.)*

8. **Interjection** — A word that expresses strong emotion.
   Example: Darn! Help! Oh!

Caution: The same word can sometimes be used as a different part of speech. The real determiner is how the word is used in a sentence.

Examples:	This is a **light** box. (adjective)
	The **light** is broken. (noun)
	Please **light** the lamp. (verb)
	He drives **fast**. (adverb)
	He is a **fast** driver. (adjective)
	The **fast** is over. (noun)

Comparative Adjectives

Adjectives (words which modify nouns) come in three forms (degrees).

Most adjectives are regular and look like this:

Positive	Comparative	Superlative
high	higher	highest
	("er" added)	("est" added)

Some adjectives are irregular and look like this:

Positive	Comparative	Superlative
good	better	best
bad	worse	worst
many	more	most
little	less	least

However, many two- (or more) syllable adjectives form the comparative and superlative by adding more/most or less/least. For example:

Positive	Comparative	Superlative
beautiful	more beautiful	most beautiful
famous	less famous	least famous
famous	more famous	most famous

SENTENCES: BASIC CONSTRUCTION

Part of grammar (rules on language use) is about different types of sentences. This is also called syntax. Here is a simplified explanation of different types of sentences:

Minimum Sentences

The basic rule is that every sentence must have a subject (noun or pronoun) and a predicate (verb). The minimum sentence looks like the following.

> Format: Subject + predicate
> *or* Noun + verb.

> Example: Birds fly.

Typical Sentences

Most sentences have another major part called the object, which comes after the verb.
> Format: Subject + predicate + object.
> *or* Noun + verb + noun.

> Example: Birds fly home.

Modifying the Subject

The subject of a sentence can be modified by adding another word or words.

> Format: Modified subject + predicate + object.
> *or* Article + adjective + adjective + noun + verb + noun.

> Example: The big black birds fly home.

Modifying the Predicate

The predicate in a sentence can be modified by adding another word or words.

> Format: Subject + modified predicate + object.
> *or* Noun + adverb + verb + noun.

> Example: Birds rapidly fly home.

Modifying the Object

The object in a sentence can be modified by adding another word or words.

> Format: Subject + predicate + modified object.
> *or* Noun + verb + preposition + adjective + noun.

> Example: Birds fly to old homes.

Modifying the Subject, Predicate, and Object

Sentences can include a combination of any of the three previous sentence parts.

> Format: Modified subject + modified predicate + modified object.

> Example: The big black birds rapidly fly to their old homes.

SENTENCES: BASIC CONSTRUCTION *(cont.)*

Negative Sentences

A sentence can say the opposite or be negative by adding a word or two like "no" or "not."

> Examples: No birds fly.
> Birds do not fly.

Questions

1. The usual way to make a sentence into a question is to put a verb in front of the subject and add a question mark at the end instead of a period.

   Example: Is he fat?

2. Questions also frequently begin with one of the five "W's" (who, what, where, when, and why) or how.

   Examples: What birds fly?
   How do birds fly?

3. Another way to make a question is to split a compound verb and put part of it before the subject.

   Examples: Can birds fly?
   Do birds fly?

Compound Sentences

Sometimes sentence can be improved by combining two short sentences into one longer sentence.

> Example: Boys go to school. Girls go to school.
> Boys and girls go to school.

"Run-On" Sentences

A run-on sentence is where two (or more) sentences are joined without punctuation or a conjunction (and, but, or). These sentences are often long or confusing but can be made more understandable by dividing them into two or more sentences.

> Run-on Sentence: The school that Trent went to won the big basketball game last year they lost almost all the games during the season.

> Correct Sentence: Trent's school won the big basketball game last year. They lost most of their games during the season.

SENTENCES: BASIC CONSTRUCTION *(cont.)*

Rambling Sentences

Sometimes a sentence is awkward because too many "and's" were used to connect ideas. This is called a rambling sentence and can be improved by breaking it into two or more sentences.

Rambling Sentence: I went home and I saw my dog and I gave him something to eat and I played with him.

Correct Sentence: When I went home and saw my dog, I gave him something to eat. Then I played with him.

Prepositional Phrases

A prepositional phrase is simply two or more words beginning with a preposition, which does not contain both a subject and a verb. A prepositional phrase can be added to a sentence in several places. In the following sentences, notice how the prepositional phrase "at night" can be put in different parts of a sentence:

Examples: Birds fly home at night.
At night, birds fly home.
Birds, at night, fly home.

The first sentence is probably the best sentence because it flows better. The second sentence is a little awkward, but appropriate if the writer wishes to stress the "night" part of the message. The third sentence may be grammatically correct, but it is awkward because it separates the subject and the verb.

Clauses

A clause is a group of words, containing a subject (noun or pronoun) and a predicate (verb), that can be added to a sentence.

Example: He took a bath before he ate dinner.

The phrase "before he ate dinner" is a dependent clause and cannot stand alone (like a sentence) because the "before" adds a condition that must be satisfied. The "He took a bath" is an independent clause and could stand alone if the writer wanted to shorten the sentence.

Paragraphs

There are few actual rules about paragraphs. The beginning of each new paragraph should be indented. When writing dialogue, use a new paragraph every time the speakers change.

Paragraphs can vary in length. Most writers today prefer short paragraphs, although some feel that one-sentence paragraphs are improper.

SENTENCES: ADVANCED CONSTRUCTION

Improving one's writing skills comes with practice. Here are some suggestions.

1. **Vary sentence length.**

   Good writers use a combination of long and short sentences.

   > Example: Short sentences have punch. Long involved sentences sometimes are necessary, but often they are harder to read and leave the reader rather confused.

2. **Vary word order.**

   The typical sentence is called a "declarative sentence" and uses the order: subject-verb-object. Variety can be added by starting with a verb phrase.

   > Before: Birds fly home after dark.

   > After: Flying home after dark is what some birds like.
   > *or* To fly home is important for some birds after dark.

3. **Use the active voice.**

   The active voice is easier to read and uses less words.

   > Examples: John read the book. (active voice)
   > The book was read by John. (passive voice)
   >
   > Rattlesnakes should not be stepped on. (passive voice)
   > Don't step on rattlesnakes. (active voice)

   There are times when the passive can be used in order to emphasize something. For example, to emphasize the "football game" instead of it being "canceled," the following passive sentence could be used.

   > Example: The football game was cancelled because of rain.

4. **Avoid negative sentences.**

   It is better to state something positively. Watch out for the word "not."

   > John did not arrive until Tuesday. (negative)
   > John arrived on Tuesday. (positive)

5. **Be concrete.**

   Use concrete examples and descriptions. Something concrete is something you can see, feel, hear, or touch.

   > Examples: The crowd was noisy. (abstract)
   > The crowd was yelling and screaming. (concrete)
   >
   > He was a big man. (abstract)
   > He was nearly seven feet tall. (concrete)

BUILD A SENTENCE

Select one from each column.

Who?	What?	Why?	When?	Where?
A boy	climbed	to see an airplane	last summer	on the moon
The shark	looked everywhere	for a vacation	in 2020	outside my house
A big dump truck	slid	to find his mother	during the game	in a cave
The monster	laughed	to get a million dollars	next year	on a farm
My Dad	swam	for fun	today	under a rock
A rattlesnake	swung on a rope	because he was on fire	at midnight	next to a lion
Maria	fell	to fall in love	forever	100 feet beneath the ocean
Mickey Mouse	yelled loudly	for an ice cream cone	before breakfast	in bed
A tiny ant	flew	to build a house	always	at the circus
The train	ran fast	to fight the enemy	500 years ago	in outer space
Iron John	jumped	to get to school	right now	downtown
A beautiful princess	kicked	to be kissed	in a month	inside an egg
A large bird	couldn't stop	for a coat of paint	after school	in Africa
My good friend	slithered	because it was mad	yesterday	out West
A teacher	hopped	on one foot	at dawn	on a tropical island

Feel free to add more words to make your sentence read better or to add interest. Remember that every sentence must have at least a subject and a verb.

VERB ERRORS

Native speakers of a language learn most verb grammar rules simply by usage. If parents speak proper English, for example, then usually their children grow up doing the same. That is the easiest way to learn grammar, but then not everyone speaks English or proper English at home. So the student must learn it in school, on the playground, or elsewhere.

There is another problem, too; written English is more formal than spoken English. When we write, we must use complete sentences, and verbs must be used correctly. Here are some helpful rules on how to avoid making verb errors.

Error Number 1: Transitive/Intransitive Verb Use

It is grammatically correct to write a simple sentence with just a subject (noun or pronoun) and a predicate (verb), such as "Birds fly." However, sentences like "Birds flew" or "The farmer milked" are incorrect. That's because there are two kinds of verbs. One kind of verb, called transitive, does not require an object (for example, "Birds fly"). The other kind, called transitive, must have an object (for example, "The birds flew south" or "The farmer milked his cow").

There is a special kind of transitive verb, called a linking verb, in which the word or words following the verb are not really an object but rather refer back to the subject (for example, "His load was heavy").

To simplify all this, let's just say: "Watch out, some verbs must have something after them."

Error Number 2: Person/Number Verb Use

It's incorrect to say: "He walk home" or "He be home." That's because verbs have to agree with the subject in terms of "person" and "number."

In English there are three persons (I, you, and he/she) and two numbers (single and plural). Here is a table of person and number for a regular verb:

	Singular	**Plural**
1st person	I walk	we walk
2nd person	you walk	you walk
3rd person	he/she/it walks	they walk

Note that the only change in the verb "walk" is in the third person singular where "walk" becomes "walks." Most English verbs follow this pattern of adding "s" or "es" to the verb whenever you use the third person singular (see "Spelling Rules" on page 76).

It is incorrect to say, "He walk home" because the third person singular requires the use of "walks."

VERB ERRORS *(cont.)*

There is one verb that is used frequently, which is irregular, and that is the verb "to be." It looks like this:

	Singular	**Plural**
1st person	I am	we are
2nd person	you are	you are
3rd person	he/she/it is	they are

Since the form for the verb "to be" in the third person singular is "is," then it is correct to say, "He is home." Sometimes people use incorrect English when speaking, and if you are writing dialogue in a story, it is acceptable to use "He be home" inside quotation marks.

Error Number 3: Past Tense

It is incorrect to say, "He walks yesterday" or "He is home yesterday" because verbs have a present tense and a past tense, which refer to time. The word "yesterday" designates the past so a past tense verb must be used with it. It would be correct to say, "He walked yesterday" or "He was home yesterday."

Here are the present and past tenses for a regular verb like "walk" and the irregular verb "to be."

	Regular Verb		**Verb "to be"**	
	Present	**Past**	**Present**	**Past**
Singular:				
1st person - I	walk	walked	am	was
2nd person - you	walk	walked	are	were
3rd person - he/she	walks	walked	is	was
Plural:				
1st person - we	walk	walked	are	were
2nd person - you	walk	walked	are	were
3rd person - they	walk	walked	are	were

Error Number 4: Future Tense

It is incorrect to say, "I walk tomorrow" or "I am home tomorrow" because verbs also have a future tense. The word "tomorrow" designates the future so a past tense verb must be used with it.

To form the future tense for a regular verb is easy; just add "will" in front of the present tense. Thus, "I will walk tomorrow" is correct. To form the future tense for the verb "to be" is a little different. The words "will be" are used for all persons, singular and plural. Thus, "I will be home tomorrow" is correct.

Most of the time in writing, either the present, the past, or the future tense will be used.

VERB ERRORS *(cont.)*

Error Number 5: Present Participle

It is incorrect to say, "He is walk home" because when the present tense of the verb "to be" is used in front of a verb, then the present participle form of the verb must be used.

Fortunately, this is very simple because most present participles are formed by simply adding the "-ing" suffix. Hence, "He is walking home" is correct.

Error Number 6: Past Participle

It is incorrect to say, "I have walk yesterday" because the past participle form is needed when the words "have," "has," or "had" are in front of the verb. The past participle form for regular verbs is easy; it is just like the past tense with an "-ed" added to the verb if it is a regular verb. Hence, "I have walked yesterday" is correct.

One difficulty with past participles is that some of them are irregular. For example, it is incorrect to say, "I have flyed before" because the verb "fly" has an irregular participle. It is correct to say, "I have flown before."

Some verbs are irregular in the past tense or in the past participle. A list of some common irregular verbs is on the next page.

Error Number 7: Boredom

Writing can be made interesting by simply using verbs that are exciting or unusual.

Boring: "He hit the ball."

Interesting: "He smashed the ball."
              "He whammed the ball."

IRREGULAR VERBS

Most verbs are regular, which means that to change from the present to the past tense usually involves adding the "-ed" suffix.

Example: walk - walked

Some verbs are irregular, however, and the past tense and/or past participle are different. (See the "Spelling Rules" section on page 76 for more discussion on verbs.)

Present	Past	Past Participle
am	was	been
are	were	been
bite	bit	bitten
catch	caught	caught
dive	dove	dived
drink	drank	drunk
do	did	done
fly	flew	flown
give	gave	given
go	went	gone
know	knew	known
put	put	put
ring	rang	rung
see	saw	seen
sing	sang	sung
steal	stole	stolen
swim	swam	swum
take	took	taken
wear	wore	worn
write	wrote	written

Here is a short summary of most of the kinds of irregular verb changes:

	Infinitive and Present	Past	Past Participle
1. Some change all forms.	give	gave	given
2. Some never change.	hit	hit	hit
3. Some have the same past tense and past participle.	hold	held	held
4. A few change past tense only.	run	ran	run

CONTRACTIONS

Contractions are two words combined to make a shorter form. An apostrophe is used to indicate any missing letter(s).

am

I'm (I am)

are

they're (they are)
we're (we are)
who're (who are)
you're (you are)

have

could've (could have)
I've (I have)
might've (might have)
should've (should have)
there've (there have)
they've (they have)
we've (we have)
who've (who have)
would've (would have)
you've (you have)

not

aren't (are not)
can't (cannot)
couldn't (could not)
doesn't (does not)
don't (do not)
hadn't (had not)
hasn't (has not)
haven't (have not)
isn't (is not)
shouldn't (should not)
wasn't (was not)
weren't (were not)
won't (will not)
wouldn't (would not)

is, has

he's (he is, has)
it's (it is, has)
she's (she is, has)
there's (there is, has)
what's (what is, has)

us

let's (let us)

will

he'll (he will)
I'll (I will)
it'll (it will)
she'll (she will)
that'll (that will)
there'll (there will)
these'll (these will)
they'll (they will)
this'll (this will)
those'll (those will)
we'll (we will)
what'll (what will)
who'll (who will)
you'll (you will)

would, had

he'd (he would, had)
I'd (I would, had)
it'd (it would, had)
she'd (she would, had)
there'd (there would, had)
they'd (they would, had)
we'd (we would, had)
what'd (what would, had)
who'd (who would, had)
you'd (you would, had)

CAPITALIZATION

All proper nouns and adjectives require capital letters. Capitalization rules are as follows.

Capitalize Proper Nouns

1. Names of people
   Examples: Bill and Mary Thomas, M.J. Beatty, George Washington

2. The pronoun I
   Example: Leslie and I are going home.

3. Titles used before a name
   Examples: Mr. Rodriguez, Dr. Lunsk, Queen Elizabeth, Mayor Sharon Knight

4. Cities, states, countries, and geographic areas
   Examples: Dallas, Indiana, United States of America, France, Southern California, the East, Lake Erie, the Pacific Ocean

5. Street names
   Examples: Hill Street, First Avenue

6. Days and months
   Examples: Thursday, April

7. School, company, and organization names
   Examples: Cawthon Elementary School, University of Illinois, Nabisco, the Red Cross, the Miami Dolphins

8. Holidays
   Examples: Christmas, Fourth of July

9. The interjection O.
   Example: How, O ye faithful companion, can I endure?

10. Religious names and all pronouns relating to the deity
    Examples: God, Jesus Christ, His, Thine; the Bible, Catholic, Allah

11. Historical events, documents, and time periods
    Examples: World War II, the Bill of Rights, the Middle Ages

12. Languages, ethnic groups, and nationalities
    Examples: Spanish, Indian, Jewish, Russian

13. Trade names
    Examples: Kleenex, Coke, Styrofoam

Capitalize the first word in a sentence.

Examples: My dog is big and shaggy. His name is Max.

Capitalize the first letter of the first word in each line of poetry.

Example: Star light, star bright,
First star I see tonight.
I wish I may, I wish I might,
Have the wish I wish tonight.

CAPITALIZATION *(cont.)*

Capitalize all main words in a title.

Examples: The new book is *The Tale of Peter Rabbit.*
Little Women was written by Louisa May Alcott.

Capitalize the first word in a quote.

Example: He said, "If I can't have it, nobody will."

Do *not* capitalize:

1. Prepositions, articles, or conjunctions in a title unless these words have over four letters or are the first word. However, always capitalize verbs, no matter how small, and "to" as part of the infinitive verb form.
Example: We heard an interesting speech, "Homework Is Without Tears: How To Make You and Your Child Choose the Right Time."

2. Seasons.
Example: The frost was a sign that winter was near.

3. Directions of the compass.
Example: Our friend's house was west of town.

4. Words in quotations if only part of the quotation is used.
Example: The principal had "mixed feelings" about the new school legislation.

5. A common (not a proper) description of a person or thing. (Remember that proper nouns — persons and titles — are capitalized.) Note the words "president" and "high school" below.

Examples: The class president was the first one at the high school prom. (common nouns)

President Jackson was the first one at Highland High School's prom. (proper nouns)

PUNCTUATION

Punctuation marks are used as follows:

Period

1. At the end of a sentence.
   Example: Birds fly.

2. After most abbreviations.
   Examples: Mr., St.

3. In decimals.
   Example: 5.95, 3.15

Question Mark

1. At the end of a question.
   Example: Who is he?

2. To express doubt.
   Example: He weighs 250 pounds?

Quotation Marks

1. To show dialogue.
   Example: She said, "Hello."

2. To indicate titles of short works, like a poem, short story, or song.
   Example: He read the poem "The Shadow."

3. To set apart special words or slang.
   Example: He is "nuts."

4. To set off direct quotes.
   Example: She told me that she "never lied."

Comma

1. To separate words or phrases in a series.
   Example: He likes candy, cake, and ice cream.

2. To separate multiple adjectives.
   Example: The big, bad, ugly wolf

3. To set off dialogue.
   Example: She said, "Hello."

4. To separate dates.
   Example: July 4, 1776

5. To enclose a title after a person's name.
   Example: Renee Andrews, Ph.D.

6. After the greeting in an informal letter.
   Example: Dear Mary,

PUNCTUATION *(cont.)*

Comma *(cont.)*

7. After the closing in a letter.
   Example: Yours truly,

8. When names are inverted.
   Example: Smith, Joe

9. To separate city and state.
   Example: Los Angeles, California,

10. To separate two independent clauses linked by a conjunction (and, but, or).
    Example: I like him, and he is tall.

11. After a dependent clause that comes before a main clause.
    Example: After the game, we went home.

12. To set off explanatory clauses.
    Example: Bill, the tall one, is here.

13. To make large numbers easier to read.
    Example: 43,126

14. To set off mild interjections.
    Examples: Yes, I will be going.
    Oh my, what happened here?

15. To separate the name of a person being addressed.
    Examples: Gretchen, please come here.
    I'm not sure about that, Keegan.

Exclamation Point

1. To show strong emotion.
   Example: She is the best!

2. After strong interjections.
   Example: Help!

Parenthesis

1. To set off supplementary material.
   Example: The map (see illustration) is good.

2. To add explanatory information.
   Example: Joe (the bad guy) is dead.

3. To enclose numbers in a list.
   Example: Her car is (1) old, (2) too slow, and (3) in need of repair.

Colon

1. To introduce a series.
   Example: He has three things: money, brains, and charm.

PUNCTUATION *(cont.)*

Colon *(cont.)*

2. To separate subtitles.
   Example: The Book: How to Read It
3. To emphasize a phrase or word.
   Example: He's not heavy: he's my brother.
4. After a business letter salutation.
   Example: Dear Sir:
5. To separate numbers in ratios and telling time.
   Examples: Mix it 3:1. It is now 7:45 A.M.

Semicolon

1. To set off independent clauses which are not linked by a conjunction.
   Example: Peace is difficult; war is hell.

2. To separate clauses containing commas.
   Example: He was tired; therefore, he quit.

Hyphen

1. To show duration.
   Examples: 1949-50, Rome-London

2. To make a compound word.
   Examples: 14-year-old student, full-time job

3. To join numbers in a fraction.
   Examples: three-fifths, one thirty-seconds

4. To combine capital letters with a noun or participle.
   Examples: T-shirt, PG-rated

5. To separate syllables in a word.
   Example: wa-ter, com-put-er

Dash

1. To emphasize a word or phrase.
   Example: The girl—the pretty one—is here.

2. To show omissions.
   Example: She called him a —.

PUNCTUATION *(cont.)*

Ellipsis

1. To show omitted words.
   Example: He...went home.

2. To indicate a pause in dialogue.
   Example: Maria and I were...uh...well, just playing.

Apostrophe

1. To show possession.

   a. For a singular possessive not ending in "s," add an apostrophe and "s."
      Examples: Bill's bike, tomorrow's jobs, the student's book

   b. For a possessive of a plural ending in "s," add only an apostrophe after the "s."
      Examples: The two students' books, Mays' farm

   c. For a possessive of the singular form of a word ending in "s," add an apostrophe after the "s" or an apostrophe and an "s."
      Example: Mrs. Cross' dog or Mrs. Cross's dog

   d. To show joint possession, add an apostrophe to the last name listed.
      Examples: John and Nancy's houses (both jointly own the houses)
      John's and Nancy's houses (each owns their own house)

   e. In compound words, add the apostrophe to the last word.
      Examples: sister-in-law's, no one else's

2. In place of omitted letters or numbers.
   Examples: isn't (is not), '59 Chevy (1959 Chevy)

3. To form the plurals of symbols, numbers, or letters.
   Examples: 1960's, three A's, two Ph.D.'s

Do *not* use an apostrophe:

1. To simply indicate plurals.
   Examples: The McKees are coming over tonight.
   The two cats are both white.

2. With the personal pronouns his, hers, its, ours, and theirs. (Note: The word "it's" is a contraction meaning "it is" or "it has.")
   Example: The purse is hers.

TYPES AND USES OF WRITING

WRITING USES

There are many uses for writing. Here is a list of some common ones and suggestions for practicing the different types of writing.

Autobiography

of myself

Biography

of my mother, friend, relative, the teacher

Directions

to my house, how to skate, care for a bike, feed a pet, make something

Invitation

to a birthday, for a dinner, to spend a weekend

Letter

to grandparent, friend, Santa Claus, the President of U.S. (business - personal - short note)

Newspaper Article

news, sports, book review, TV review, movie review, play review

Poems (rhyme or nonrhyme)

about a friend, death, home, farm, mountain, lake;

Report

for science, for social studies

Stories

fact - fantasy - opinion
family - travel
fiction - nonfiction
humorous - serious
mystery - adventure
short - long

THANK YOU NOTE OR FRIENDLY LETTER FORM

When you receive a gift or someone does you a favor, it is courteous to write a thank you note. Usually, it is short and follows the form of a friendly letter, which is shown below.

Heading	*167 George Road* *Columbus, NJ 08022* *January 12, 2000*
Greeting	*Dear Aunt June,*
Body	*Thank you for the green gift. You are right. It is my favorite color! Yesterday, I went to the mall and bought some video tapes. Next time you come over, I'll show them to you and thank you in person.*
Closing **Signature**	*Your nephew,* *Zach*

A thank you note starts with a **heading** that states your address and the date. Be sure to put a comma between the city and state and also between the day of the month and the year.

The first word of the **greeting** is usually "Dear." Notice that it begins with a capital letter. The second part of the greeting is the name of the person to whom the letter is being written. It is followed by a comma.

The part of the note where you say thank you is called the **body**. In a friendly letter, this is where you write your news or message. The first word of every paragraph is indented.

The **closing** shows who wrote the note. Notice that only the first word is capitalized, and a comma follows the last word. Often the words "Sincerely," or "Yours truly," are used as a closing.

The closing lines up with the heading and **signature,** which is your name. Typically, this is just your first name.

BUSINESS LETTER FORM

To order something through the mail, ask for permission, or obtain information, you need to write a business letter. It is different from a friendly letter in terms of format and is also much more formal. There is an inside address and the punctuation after the greeting is different.

Heading

> *320 20th Avenue*
> *Menomonie, WI 54751*
> *April 21, 2000*

Inside Address

> *Ms. Heather Kistler, Director*
> *Arkansas Department of Tourism*
> *Box 1107*
> *Little Rock, AR 72201*

Greeting

> *Dear Ms. Kistler:*

Body

> *My family is planning on taking a camping trip this summer. Please send me a state map and some information about campgrounds and what places to see.*
>
> *Right now we are interested in the Hot Springs National Park area. Information about other interesting parts of the state will help us decide what else to visit.*

Closing
Signature

> *Yours truly,*
> *Kara Zola*

A business letter starts with a **heading**. It gives your address and the date. Notice that there is a comma between the city and state and also between the day of the month and the year.

The **inside address** gives the name, title, and address of the person to whom you are writing as well as the name of the company. Put a comma between the person's name and title, and capitalize the person's title.

The **greeting** in a business letter is followed by a colon (:). Then comes the **body** or content of the letter.

In the **closing**, only the first word is capitalized. A business letter can close with "Respectfully," "Sincerely," or "Yours truly." A comma follows the last word.

The closing and the **signature**, which is the writer's name, line up with the heading. Add your position (or title) after the signature if it is appropriate.

> Example: Joe Smith
> Asst. Manager

Add enclosures, if there are any, at the bottom after the signature.

> Example: Enclosed, 2 photographs.

BOOK REPORT FORM

In a book report, tell what a book is about and also give your opinion of it. The form below will help you by giving questions or comments that should be discussed in each section. Remember to use complete sentences.

_____

Title (Underline, center, and capitalize all important words.)

_____

Author (Center and write the author's first and last name.)

(Tell what the book is about by answering, when appropriate, the questions: Who? What? Where? When? Why? How?)

_____
_____
_____
_____
_____
_____

(Who is your favorite or least favorite character? Why? When?)

_____
_____
_____

(What is your opinion of the book? Why?)

_____
_____
_____

(Do you recommend this book? If so, to whom? Why?)

_____
_____
_____

STORY SUMMARIZING FORM

Often you are asked to summarize or retell a story. The following form shows all the parts of a story and is called a story map. If you write about each story part, your summary will be complete.

When writing a story, you can use this same form to help plan what to say.

Story Map

Title: _____

Characters (main character and/or other major characters): _____

_____

_____

Setting: _____

_____

_____

_____

Problem: _____

_____

_____

Events (or plan):

1. _____

2. _____

3. _____

Outcome (or result): _____

_____

_____

_____

KEEPING A DAILY JOURNAL

A daily journal is like a diary. The difference is that you do not write anything secret or private in it, the way you might in a diary. Many writers view a journal as their best friend. It's a place where you can:

- jot down an idea.
- experiment with writing.
- write a creative story or poem.
- expand your vocabulary by writing down new words you like.
- practice writing everyday.
- record an impression of the weather.
- write how you feel at a particular time.
- tell your reaction to what is happening around you.
- write down an opinion of a book, a movie, or music.

Your recorded thoughts can also serve as a source of ideas for writing at a later time. Often you will write about things in your journal that you want to share with others.

Tips for Writing in Your Journal

1. Date each entry.

2. Begin by writing three to five minutes a day. Move up gradually to 10 minutes a day.

3. Write when you feel relaxed, if possible.

4. Don't worry about spelling or punctuation. The important thing is that you are writing and getting ideas down on paper.

5. If doing creative writing, you could use one of the ideas in the following section "Things to Write About in Your Journal," or you might like to use one of the "Story Starters" ideas (see pages 132–135).

6. Write in complete sentences when you put down your thoughts.

7. Use action verbs and the present tense to keep your writing lively.

8. Use adjectives and adverbs to give a clearer picture.

KEEPING A DAILY JOURNAL *(cont.)*

Things to Write About in Your Journal

1. Write about your hobby or something you would like to do as a hobby.

2. Tell about the history of your city or state.

3. Relate what the best thing about living today is. The worst thing.

4. Describe what pictures come to mind when you think about nature.

5. Write a poem about a sunrise, a sunset, or anything that interests you.

6. Find a picture that you like. React to it in your journal.

7. Write about something you have just learned about.

8. Tell how schools today are different from when your grandparents went to school.

9. Describe your favorite quiet place and tell what you think about when you are there.

10. Write about a beach or lakeshore near where you live. What have you found when you have combed the beach?

THE WRITING PROCESS

There are a lot of different kinds of writing. Sometimes you write for other people, such as a note to a friend. Sometimes you write for yourself, perhaps in a daily journal or just a note to remind yourself about something you have to do.

Sometimes you write quickly, without giving the words or the order of the ideas too much thought. Then there are times when you want to write something good enough to share with other people. That is the time when you need to use the step-by-step guidelines in "The Writing Process." There are four stages: prewriting, writing, revising, and proofreading.

Few people write well on the first try. It takes time. Time is needed to think, to plan, to gather ideas (Stage One: Prewriting). After you have written (Stage Two: Writing), you need more time to review it. Then time is needed for changes (Stage Three: Revising) and for corrections (Stage Four: Proofreading). Some ideas that will help during each of the four stages are given on the pages that follow.

STAGE 1: PREWRITING
"Get Ready To Write"

Most writers do not know what they want to say before they begin. They need to take time to get ideas. Here are some things to try.

1. **Brainstorm** by yourself, with a partner, or several others.

2. Fold a piece of paper into four **sections.** Then write a thought that goes with the topic you are writing about. After you have filled in each section, go back and put a number on each part. Put a "1" before the idea you should write about first, then a "2" before the next idea in order, and so on. If you used both sides of the sheet, you will have eight sections numbered. (Many students do this when they answer essay questions on tests.)

3. **Interview** someone. It might be a parent, a teacher, a student, or someone in the community. Prepare a list of questions in advance. When the person being interviewed answers your questions, he or she will trigger some additional thoughts in your head on the topic you selected. Talking to someone else usually helps you prepare to write. Often two heads really are better than one.

4. Keep a **journal** and carry it with you while working on a writing project. Jot down ideas when they come to your mind. If you happen to see something that relates to your topic, record your impressions right away. Try to write in the journal every day. It might be an idea, an opinion, or an impression. When you have to come up with an original idea for something to write about, you probably will be able to find a topic here. Also, keeping a journal will provide you with practice in expressing yourself with words. It will give you a chance to experiment with writing. (See the "Story Starters" on pages 132–135 for some story ideas.)

STAGE 1: PREWRITING *(cont.)*

5. Write an important word or idea on a page, and draw a circle around it. Then cluster other related words on the same page. By the time you have finished filling up the paper with words that go with the original circled word or idea, you will have many thoughts to write about. This is called **clustering.**

Here is an example of a student's clustering around the topic "bread."

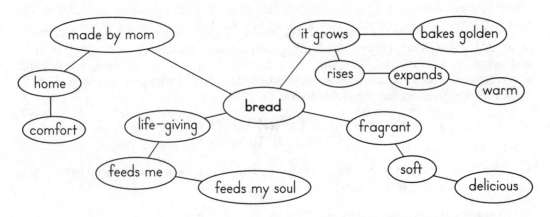

There is no set pattern for how a cluster grows. Ideas can be connected in any way. Here is a paragraph written from the information above.

Bread is my favorite food. Its warm, fragrant welcome brings me home. It is love from my mom as she slices a piece for me. It's soft and delicious and gives me life. I like to see how it grows in the pan and then bakes until golden. Bread is my favorite food. It feeds me while it feeds my soul.

STAGE 2: WRITING
"Put Your Ideas On Paper"

After you have gone through the prewriting stage, you have a topic to write about and some notes. That's a good start, but what do you do about that empty piece of paper in front of you? That's easy — just start writing! Now is the time to get your ideas down on paper. The words will probably not all be spelled right, and some of your ideas will be out of order. Do not be concerned about that at this point. In the revising and proofreading stages, you will improve what you have written and correct any mistakes. Write on every other line at this stage, so you will have plenty of room to make changes later.

Try one of the following ideas to get you started or help you continue to write.

1. Write a title for or a phrase about your topic on a sheet of paper. Then list the first 10 words that pop into your mind. Choose any **three words** of those 10, and use them in your first sentence. Finally, expand that sentence by explaining it throughout the rest of the paragraph. If your topic is "Buying a Gift," you might quickly list "bathrobe," "purple," "department store," "mortician," "long," "pole," "steps," "crumpled," "sadly," and "broken." The three you select might be "bathrobe," "department store," and "mortician." When you create the topic sentence, you might come up with:

> *The town's mortician went into its largest department store looking for a bathrobe. At first, the salesclerk who waited on him thought that nothing was unusual. But after showing Mr. Dragonne every bathrobe in stock, she began to feel uneasy. Why didn't he leave? Why didn't he go to another store? Or why didn't he ask her to order one that she had in a different size? Mr. Dragonne seemed to be taking his time. He talked very slowly, and he moved very slowly. The salesclerk became more and more nervous.*

If you cannot think of what to write for the second paragraph, select a word or idea related to the first paragraph you have just written. List 10 more words very quickly, without thinking. Pick three of them, and write the first sentence of the second paragraph. Then write more about that first sentence to complete the second paragraph.

STAGE 2: WRITING *(cont.)*

2. Ask a **question** at the beginning of your writing. During the prewriting stage, you may have observed something carefully, perhaps a dog scratching himself, and made notes on it. Read over your notes and come up with a question that you can begin your writing with, such as "Did you ever notice how a dog scratches himself?" Then use your notes to describe what happens. You may not have to use all the notes you took. Just use the best details that you noted. Finally, add an "ending sentence," such as "We should have named him Itchy!"

3. Begin by making a **statement about a character.** For example, you could say, "There was a big bully with bright red hair who liked to chase his classmates home from school."

4. Begin by having the **main character speak.** For example, you might write: "Ha! Scared you again! I love to chase scaredy cats," said the red-haired bully.

5. Open with **your opinion.** Write it as though you were talking to a friend. You could begin with a sentence like this: "David, someday you should try to be pleasant to your classmates. Have you ever thought about sharing the dessert your mother packs in your lunch each day?"

6. Start with a **simile.** Compare unlike things using the words "like" or "as." You might write: "The school stands like a fort." "His hair was as bright as a stoplight." (See "Jazz Up Your Writing Style" on pages 137–141 for additional ideas.)

7. When you don't know where to begin or what to say next, you have what is called writer's block. One way to break the "block" is to **write your name over and over.** Do that until an idea pops into your mind. You will be surprised at how quickly another idea will come when you keep your writing hand moving.

8. Another way to break a writer's block is to **rearrange** what you have already written. Often the place where you are stuck is not really the problem. You may have made a wrong turn a few paragraphs back, and now you are at a dead end. The only way out of a dead end is to go back to the place where you made the wrong turn. By rearranging what you are writing, you can find the place that is causing trouble.

9. Writing **does not have to be done in order** from beginning to end. Sometimes it is easier to write the end or the middle before the beginning. Begin wherever you can. You can always rearrange later.

STAGE 3: REVISING

"Improve Your Writing by Making Changes"

Reading to yourself is an important step in revising. Ask yourself if you have met your purpose. Think about the audience. Will they understand your message? You will probably need to cross out some words and write in new ones. Maybe you will want to draw arrows to show where words or sentences should be moved. Revisions are often done in another color pencil or ink. Don't worry about your writing looking messy at this point. You will make it look neat again later.

Next, read what you have written to a partner. Ask him or her what part was best and if there was anything he or she would like to know more about. Ask if the sequential order is correct. Find out if your partner can offer any suggestions. Then make more changes if you think they will improve what you have written. Compare what you have written to the revision checklist below.

Revision Checklist

_____ **1. Did I meet my purpose? Some possibilities are listed.**

_____ Did I write about something that happened to me?

_____ Did I tell about something I can do?

_____ Did I try to persuade someone to try something?

_____ Did I try to persuade someone to buy something?

_____ Did I get across my vision of something?

_____ Did I explain how to do something?

_____ Did I write a biography of a real person?

_____ Did I write a description of something?

_____ Did I write a fairy tale, fable, or fantasy?

_____ Did I write a humorous story?

_____ Did I compare two things?

_____ Did I write a poem?

_____ Did I describe something, like my favorite food?

_____ Other

_____ **2. Will my audience respond to what I have written?**

_____ Will they understand?

_____ Will they enjoy it?

_____ Will they be persuaded?

_____ Will they be able to follow the steps?

STAGE 3: REVISING *(cont.)*

_____   3. Is what I have written in order?

_____   4. Did I include interesting facts and as well as facts that readers would like to know (if appropriate)?

_____   5. Did I give facts and reasons to support my opinion (if appropriate)?

_____   6. If I wrote about two things, did I tell how they are alike?

_____   7. If I wrote about two things, did I tell how they are different?

_____   8. If I wrote about two things, did I use any similes or metaphors?

_____   9. Are there more exact or stronger words that I could use? (A thesaurus is a good place for finding other words with similar meanings.)

_____   10. Did I overuse any words? (Look in a thesaurus to find more interesting words.)

_____   11. Did I put too many ideas in one sentence? Can I improve a sentence by making two or more shorter sentences?

_____   12. Did I keep my sentences short enough? (Usually, the shorter the sentence, the easier it is to read.)

_____   13. Did I avoid using too many short sentences so that my writing does not sound choppy?

_____   14. Did I use different kinds of sentences, such as exclamatory or interrogatory, to make my writing interesting?

_____   15. Did I use positive words? (Positive sentences are easier to understand than negative ones. Not this: We can't go until Monday. But this: We can go Monday.)

_____   16. Have I used the same nouns and verbs too often? Can I replace a repeated word with one that means the same?

_____   17. Can I replace some nouns with pronouns to add variety?

_____   18. Are some sentences fuzzy? (If you replace too many nouns with pronouns, some sentences will become unclear.)

_____   19. Did I use "I" and "me" correctly?

_____   20. Do the verbs agree with the subjects of the sentences?

STAGE 3: REVISING *(cont.)*

_____ 21. **Was I careful when forming the past tense of irregular verbs?**

_____ 22. **Are all the verbs in the same tense (the same time)?**

_____ 23. **Did I overuse common adjectives, such as "good," "bad," and "nice"?**

_____ 24. **Do adjectives add details and help form sharp word pictures?**

_____ 25. **Did I use adverbs to give information about "how," "when," and "where" and to make my meaning more clear?**

_____ 26. **Was I careful not to start any sentences with the conjunctions "and" or "but"?**

STAGE 4: PROOFREADING
"Find and Fix the Errors"

Now that you have checked to see that what you have written says what you want it to say, it is time to proofread it. By proofreading, you are making it easier for the reader to read and understand what you have written.

Look for only one type of error at a time. For example, you might look for spelling errors first. Later you can look for other errors in capitalizing, punctuating, and indenting.

When proofreading, it is a good idea to put a sheet of paper or a ruler under each line as you read it. That way you will be more likely to find any mistakes. It is easier to find spelling errors if you read each line backward or read only every other word and then go back to check the words you skipped. That way you think about each word separately instead of the meaning of the whole sentence or paragraph.

Perhaps you can find someone to read what you have written. It is usually easier to spot someone else's mistakes. Maybe you can read the other person's work and help each other fix mistakes. When proofreading someone else's writing, circle any errors.

If you find a error in your own writing, use a proofreading mark. Often a red pen or pencil is used so that the marks will stand out. A list of proofreading marks is on the next page. The proofreading checklist below will help you to find your errors, too.

Proofreading Checklist

_____ 1. **Did I spell words correctly? (Use the "Spelling Checklist" or pages 11–68.)**

_____ 2. **Did I capitalize correctly? (See "Capitalization" on pages 110–111.)**

_____ 3. **Did I indent each paragraph?**

_____ 4. **Did I use the correct punctuation mark at the end of each sentence?**

STAGE 4: PROOFREADING *(cont.)*

_____	5.	Did I put commas in the right places? (See "Punctuation" on pages 112–115.)
_____	6.	Did I use clear, readable handwriting?
_____	7.	Did I dot every "i" and cross every "t"?
_____	8.	Did I leave the right amount of space between each word so that the words are not crowded?
_____	9.	Did I space the letters so that each can be clearly seen?
_____	10.	Is there a little extra space between each sentence?
_____	11.	Does every sentence have a noun and a verb? (See "Sentences: Basic Construction" on pages 100–102.)

Sharing

After proofreading, give an interesting title to what you have written, copy it very neatly, and share your writing with others. You could read it aloud, record it on an audio tape, or maybe put your writing on a bulletin board for others to see and enjoy. An important part of writing is getting a response from an audience, so share what you have written!

PROOFREADING SYMBOLS

Teachers and editors often use the following symbols to indicate how to correct errors or improve the writing.

Notation in Margin	How Indicated in Copy	Explanation
¶	true. The best rule to follow	new paragraph
⌒	living room	close up
#	Mary hada	insert space
∼	May had a lamb little	transpose
sp	There were 5 children	spell out
cap	mary had a little lamb	capitalize
lc	Mary had a little Lamb	lowercase
e	The correct proceduree	delete or take out
stet	Mary had a little lamb	restore crossed-out word(s)
little	Mary had a lamb	insert word(s) in margin
⊙	Birds fly	insert a period
⌃,	Next the main	insert a comma

INTERESTING TITLES

Do you need a title for a story? Here are some from which to choose.

- The Me That Nobody Knows
- The Tallest Tale of All
- My Best Quality
- The Perfect Gift
- The Turquoise Airplane
- The Elephant Without Ears
- The Giraffe Without a Neck
- The Machine That Came Alive
- The Big Wish
- The Sleeping Guard
- The Big White Lie
- The Giant Shrimp
- In the Dark
- The Super-Duper Market
- The Farm in the City
- The Lost Suitcase
- The Sleeping Night
- The Day Without Sunshine
- The Circus Came to Town
- The Troll Under the Bridge
- The Visitor at Midnight
- Vitamin Soup
- The Disappearing Backpack
- The Web
- The Whimpering Puppy
- The Wacky Weekend

OPENING SENTENCES

Every story needs an opening that will catch the interest of readers. Try one of these sentences to get started.

- I won't be attending school for the rest of the year because...
- My favorite childhood toy was...
- My favorite teacher is...because...
- If I could be any animal in the zoo, I would be...
- I gave a classmate some garlic-flavored chewing gum because...
- The best day of my life was when...
- The worst day of my life was when...
- If I could be anybody, I'd like to be...
- If I were invited to write for a television show, I'd write scripts for...
- When I raise children, I'll never...
- Ten (or as many as you can think of) uses for a pillowcase are...
- The thunder and lightning frightened me so much that I...
- The nonsense word "nooeaia" means...
- A blue monster got on the bus and...
- I had a nightmare about...
- My goal in life is to...
- I just bought a new...
- My favorite time of day is...
- When the sun came up, I...
- My favorite song makes me feel...
- I like the music group (your favorite) because...
- If I were a teacher, I would...
- The flowers suddenly bloomed when...
- When the door burst open,...
- My favorite possession is...
- My favorite author is...
- My favorite book is...
- The most exciting thing that ever happened at school was...
- The last movie I saw was...
- My favorite comic strip character is...
- I would like to be...
- Holidays (or name a specific holiday) make(s) me feel...
- I can hardly wait to...

GREAT QUESTIONS

Sometimes a question can give you an idea for a story. Here are some that may inspire you.

- Where do lost socks and gloves go?
- What piece of furniture am I most like? Why?
- Who would I like to look like? Why? What would I do differently if I looked like that person?
- What character in a book would you like to meet? Why?
- What will you be when you are an adult?
- In what century would you like to live?
- If you couldn't live on Earth, on what planet would you go to live? Why?
- What words have you invented? Why? What do they mean?
- Did you ever take a plane trip by yourself? Where? Why?
- What is it like sitting next to you in the school cafeteria?
- What do you think the class president will be doing in twenty years?
- Why do you like to talk on the phone to your best friend?
- If you could change your house, what would it be like?
- What might happen today that would make you very happy or very sad?
- What is an average day in your life like?
- Where would you rather live?
- What does the moon think about the sun?
- What do the clouds think about the airplanes?
- Why do the stars twinkle so brightly?
- What is your favorite fairy tale? Why?
- What is your favorite cartoon? Why?
- Why has the hair on only one side of your head been cut off?
- What would you do if you were a giant?
- How would one of your parents describe you?
- If you were a teacher, how would you handle a student who misbehaves?
- What is your favorite after-school activity?
- What would you do if you were served purple spinach?
- What would you do today if you could do anything you wanted?
- How do you care for the classroom pet?
- What would you pack for a trip to Disney World?
- What commercial don't you like? Why?

STORY ENDINGS

All stories need the right ending. Here are some ideas.

- I have never in my life been more frightened.
- We had to buy it even though we really didn't want it anymore.
- That finally persuaded me to give up chocolate.
- Then they charged me five dollars.
- That is a day I'd like to forget.
- It was a day I'll always remember.
- Now it is a common saying among my friends/family.
- It has changed my life forever.
- Now he/she is my favorite hero/heroine.
- That's the last time I'll ever play hide and seek.
- It cost a lot of money, but it was worth it.
- It was the right choice.
- Obviously, I made the wrong choice.
- Then the lights went out.
- That's why they named the town Cleverville.
- Now my friends say I could be a cartoon hero/heroine.
- Everything he had said was an exaggeration.
- To this day, I won't eat that food.
- It was the best smell in the world.
- Now you can understand why I was so mad.
- That was the end of a perfect week.
- We'll never go back there again.
- Even though I felt tired, it was a job well done.
- They don't think of me as just a kid anymore.
- It was the worst vacation we ever had.
- Finally, we had to let it go.

TIPS ON IMPROVING YOUR VOCABULARY

Writers notice and collect words. That's because words are what make a story; they can make it funny, sad, exciting, scary, and more. The following are some tips to help expand your vocabulary and make your writing more interesting.

1. Start a word bank. Decorate a coffee can, a small box, or an envelope. Also cut some 3" x 5" (8 cm x 13 cm) index cards into smaller cards. Whenever you come across a word that interests you, write it on a small card and put it in the word bank. You also may want to write the meaning of the word on the back of the card along with a sentence using the word.

2. Nouns are words used to name a person, place, or thing. In writing, they help create word pictures. Look around and observe some of the "nouns" around you. Write them (especially less common ones) on small word cards and add them to your word bank.

3. Some nouns name certain groups of things and are called collective nouns. Some examples are: colony of ants, crowd of people, fleet of taxicabs, flock of sheep, gaggle of geese, herd of cattle, pride of lions, and swarm of mosquitoes. Can you think of others? Add them to your word bank, and use them where they fit.

4. Action verbs tell what happens to the subject. Look in your journal and list 10 action verbs. Trade your list with a partner. Use each other's action verbs in sentences. Also write them on word cards.

5. Some words echo the sounds they name, such as "buzz," "crash," "flop," and "zoom." Listen to the sounds around you. Make a list of other words that sound like the things they name. Add them to your word bank.

6. Trade writing assignments or stories with a classmate. Find his or her adjectives and/or adverbs. Add ones that interest you to your word bank.

7. Reread the last thing you wrote. List the verbs, nouns, pronouns, adverbs, adjectives, and conjunctions in separate columns. Add any interesting or unusual words to your word bank.

LITERARY TERMS

The following is a list of literary terms, which can add a new element or a bit of sparkle to your writing. These terms may suggest an element of style that you seldom use but perhaps ought to (at least on occasion).

alliteration — Alliteration occurs when two or more words have the same beginning sound.

> Example: Mike mixed some malt in his milk.

antithesis — Contrasting words or ideas by asserting something and denying its contrary or by parallel or balanced phrases.

> Example: This soup should be eaten cold, not hot.

antonym — This is a word or expression that means the opposite or near the opposite of another word or expression. (In fact, the opposite of an antonym is a synonym.) For example, "come - go" and "up - down" are antonyms. Antonyms are sometimes used for emphasis when writing.

> Examples: "I mean up, not down." "Mother didn't ask him to work, she told him to work."

Here are a few antonyms:

clean - dirty	**North - South**
first - last	**old - young**
good - bad	**then - now**
large - small	**top - bottom**

cohesion — Cohesion refers to how well a story or article fits together. This can be determined by seeing if the parts connect to the whole and how much one part relates to another part. For example, an article or story would have cohesion if sentences or paragraphs refer to an earlier part of the article or story. Also see signal words and story structures.

dialogue — A dialogue is a conversation between characters in a story or play. When you change speakers, each speaker is a new paragraph. Quotation marks set off the actual dialogue.

> Example: He said, "I'll be home tonight."

fact — A fact is a statement that can be proven.

> Example: There are about four million children at each grade level.

fantasy — Fantasy is a story that has imagined characters, settings, or other elements that could never really exist.

> Examples: Mickey Mouse or spiders that talk.

LITERARY TERMS *(cont.)*

flashback — A break in the chronological sequence where an earlier incident is described.

homonyms — These are words that have the same sound and often the same spelling but have different meanings.

> Examples: We saw a **bear** in the woods. (type of animal)
> Our cat will soon **bear** kittens. (give birth to)

homophones — These are words that sound the same but have different meanings and different spellings. They are important to beginning writers because they often cause many spelling errors. The following are some common homophones, their meanings, and examples.

Homophones	Definitions	Examples
ate	(to eat)	She **ate** half the pizza.
eight	(the number 8)	He has **eight** baseballs.
eye	(used to see with)	She got sand in her **eye**.
I	(myself)	**I** don't like it.
hour	(time)	The lesson takes an **hour**.
our	(belonging to us)	He lives on **our** street.
know	(familiar with)	He did not **know** how to spell it.
no	(negative)	She said, "**No**, I will not go."
their	(belonging to them)	It is **their** book.
there	(a place)	Put the book over **there**.
they're	(they are)	**They're** not going to play.
to	(in the direction of)	I went **to** school.
too	(also)	My dog went to school, **too**.
two	(the number 2)	Pedro is in grade **two**.

hyperbole — A hyperbole is an exaggeration.

> Example: He must have been nine feet tall.

idiom — An expression that cannot be understood from the literal meaning of the words is an idiom.

> Example: Tom is barking up the wrong tree.

imagery — Imagery is where a writer uses descriptive words to create a vivid picture or image in the reader's mind.

> Example: A blanket of soft snow covered the sleeping woods.

LITERARY TERMS *(cont.)*

irony — This is the use of tone, exaggeration, or understatement to express the opposite of the literal meaning of the words used. (Irony can be related to sarcasm.)

> Example: I didn't mind waiting two hours; it was restful.

litotes — Litotes is an understatement or assertion made by denying or negating its opposite.

> Example: He wasn't unhappy about winning the bet.

metaphor — A metaphor is the comparison of two things, using an object to describe someone or something.

> Example: His feet are like boats.

There are different kinds of metaphors:

- **abstract metaphor** — Links an abstract concept with an object.

  > Example: Death is the pits.

- **animal metaphor** — Associates the characteristics of an animal with a human or object.

  > Example: What a teddy bear he is!

- **frozen metaphor** — A frozen metaphor is one that has been so frequently used that it has become an idiom or an expression commonly understood, but without a literal meaning.

  > Example: head of the class

- **humanistic metaphor** — Gives inanimate objects human qualities or humans inanimate qualities.

  > Examples: A user-friendly computer, her porcelain skin

- **inanimate metaphor** — Pairs the quality of an inanimate object with another inanimate object.

  > Example: The walls were paper thin.

- **incarnation metaphor** — This links the attributes of a deceased person to another person or entity.

  > Example: He is a modern George Washington.

- **sense metaphor** — A sense metaphor relates one of the five senses to an object or situation.

  > Example: a cool reception

LITERARY TERMS *(cont.)*

metonymy — Metonymy is the use of a related word in place of what is really being talked about.

Examples: "pen" instead of "write" or "dry" instead of "thirsty"

news article — Articles in a newspaper or periodical often follow the format where the five basic questions (who, what, where, when, and why) are answered in the first sentence or paragraph. In news articles, paragraphs are usually short and the information is factual, not opinions.

onomatopoeia — Onomatopoeia are words in which the sounds suggest the meaning of the words.

Examples: ouch, bang, bow-wow, drip, oink, crash

opinion — An opinion is a statement of someone's idea or feelings. An opinion cannot be proven although it can be based on facts. Newspaper editorials, book and movie reviews, and signed columns are types of writing which contain opinions.

Example: George is the best candidate.

personification — Linking a human quality or ability to an animal, object, or idea is called personification.

Examples: The wind whispered through the night. Our school is friendly.

point of view — Point of view refers to how a story is narrated. If it is narrated from the first person point of view, the narrator is a character in the story and uses first person pronouns (I, me, mine, we, and our). If the story is narrated from the third person point of view, the narrator is not part of the story and uses third person pronouns (he, him, she, her, and them).

prediction — Making a prediction is to tell about, or make known beforehand, based on knowledge or special information.

Example: The world will be overcrowded in 2040.

setting — The time and place in which a story happens is called the setting.

Example: She lived in England in the last century.

signal words — These words refer to the story structure or cohesion, but more specifically, they tell the reader that something is coming up or the next part is somehow related. Here are some specific kinds of signal words:

1. **continuation signal** — Examples: and, in addition, also
2. **change of direction signals** — Examples: but, however, in contrast
3. **sequence signals** — Examples: next, second, since, later
4. **illustration signals** — Examples: for example, to illustrate, such as
5. **emphasis signals** — Examples: remember that, the key feature, most important

LITERARY TERMS *(cont.)*

6. **cause, condition, or result signals** — Example: if, while, due to, because

7. **spatial signals** — Examples: under, between, on, close to

8. **comparison-contrast signals** — Examples: less than, different from, same

9. **conclusion signals** — Examples: in conclusion, in summary, therefore

10. **fuzz signals** — Examples: if, maybe, could, looks like, probably

11. **nonword emphasis signals** — Examples: exclamation point, underline, subheads

simile — A simile is a comparison of two things using the words "like" or "as." (Similes are a type of metaphor. See "metaphor" for types.)

Example: She felt as limp as a rag doll.

story structures — There are a lot of ways to structure stories. Here is a short list of some different kinds of story structures.

1. **cause and effect**
2. **sequence or chronological order**
3. **comparison or contrast**
4. **statements and conclusions**
5. **conflict and resolution**
6. **description**
7. **main idea and detail**
8. **problem and solution**
9. **theme, essay, academic discussion of a topic**
10. **news article**
11. **mystery story—surprise ending**

synonyms — A synonym is a word or phrase (short group of words) that means the same or about the same as another word. For example, "like" and "enjoy" mean about the same thing. However, since a lot of words have several meanings, be sure that you use a synonym that means what you want to say.

Plain Sentence: He said, "She likes me."
With synonyms: The big guy whispered, "She really enjoys my company."

Here are a few synonyms:

> **night = evening, dark, after sunset**
> **boy = guy, fellow, young man, child, student**
> **said = yelled, asked, whispered, called**

Many dictionaries have synonyms as part of the definition or in a separate list. A "thesaurus" is a whole book of synonyms.

INDEX

INDEX *(cont.)*

INDEX *(cont.)*